ARCHITECTURAL DESIGN

GUEST-EDITED BY
MICHAEL WEINSTOCK

SYSTEM CITY
INFRASTRUCTURE AND THE SPACE OF FLOWS

04|2013

ARCHITECTURAL DESIGN
JULY/AUGUST 2013
ISSN 0003-8504

PROFILE NO 224
ISBN 978-1118-361429

ARCHITECTURAL DESIGN

GUEST-EDITED BY
MICHAEL WEINSTOCK

SYSTEM CITY: INFRASTRUCTURE AND THE SPACE OF FLOWS

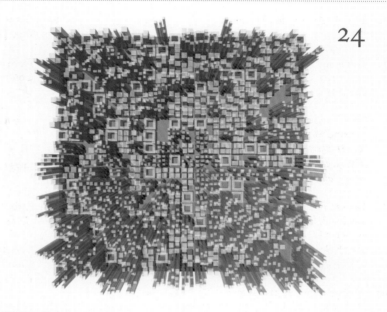

24

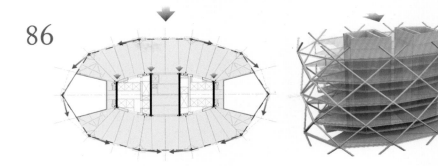

86

The city is critical to the capacity of society to adapt to a future of uncertainty and change.
— *Michael Weinstock*

106

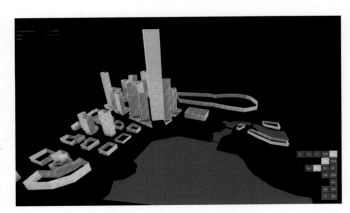

ARCHITECTURAL DESIGN
JULY/AUGUST 2013
PROFILE NO 224

Editorial Offices
John Wiley & Sons
25 John Street
London WC1N 2BS
UK

T: +44 (0)20 8326 3800

Editor
Helen Castle

Managing Editor (Freelance)
Caroline Ellerby

Production Editor
Elizabeth Gongde

Prepress
Artmedia, London

Art Direction and Design
CHK Design:
Christian Küsters
Sophie Troppmair

Printed in Italy by Printer Trento Srl

Sponsorship/advertising
Faith Pidduck/Wayne Frost
T: +44 (0)1243 770254
E: fpidduck@wiley.co.uk

Subscribe to ⚖

⚖ is published bimonthly and is
available to purchase on both a
subscription basis and as individual
volumes at the following prices.

Prices
Individual copies: £24.99/ US$45
Individual issues on ⚖ App
for iPad: £9.99/ US$13.99
Mailing fees for print may apply

Annual Subscription Rates
Student: £75 / US$117 print only
Personal: £120 / US$189 print and
iPad access
Institutional: £212 / US$398 print
or online
Institutional: £244 / US$457
combined print and online
6-issue subscription on ⚖ App
for iPad: £44.99/ US$64.99

Subscription Offices UK
John Wiley & Sons Ltd
Journals Administration Department
1 Oldlands Way, Bognor Regis
West Sussex, PO22 9SA, UK
T: +44 (0)1243 843 272
F: +44 (0)1243 843 232
E: cs-journals@wiley.co.uk

Print ISSN: 0003-8504
Online ISSN: 1554-2769

Prices are for six issues and include
postage and handling charges.
Individual-rate subscriptions must be
paid by personal cheque or credit card.
Individual-rate subscriptions may not
be resold or used as library copies.

All prices are subject to change
without notice.

Rights and Permissions
Requests to the Publisher should be
addressed to:
Permissions Department
John Wiley & Sons Ltd
The Atrium
Southern Gate
Chichester
West Sussex PO19 8SQ
UK

F: +44 (0)1243 770 620
E: permreq@wiley.co.uk

Front, back and inside front cover: Mehran
Gharleghi, Model of the City, AA Emergent
Technologies and Design (EmTech), Architectural
Association, 2013–14. © Michael Weinstock

EDITORIAL
Helen Castle

The 'system city' represents a whole-scale rethink of the urban. In recent years, the reach and influence of large-scale cities has tended to be traced on socioeconomic grounds as reflected by Saskia Sassen's coining of the 'global city',[1] or in terms of demographics with the 'megacity' label being applied to cities with over 10 million inhabitants.[2] In this issue of ⚰, Guest-Editor Michael Weinstock places the urban on a much wider canvas – whether at the evolutionary, cultural or global scale. He pushes at the envelope of the current notion of the city, where the city's relationship to the global is largely regarded in terms of 'connectivity' to the Internet or worldwide trade. Weinstock's concept advances to an entirely new holistic level: 'Considering the city as a dynamic complex system places emphasis on the interactions and connectivity of the flows through its infrastructures, and of the feedbacks and critical thresholds that drive the emergence of new spaces and urban morphologies that are animated by new modalities of culture' (see p 17). He brings a scientific lens informed by his work on 'emergence' at the Architectural Association (AA) School of Architecture in London, where he is a co-founder and co-director of the Emergent Technologies and Design (EmTech) Masters programme. As part of this project he co-guest-edited, with Michael Hensel and Achim Menges, the seminal ⚰ issues *Emergence: Morphogenetic Design Strategies* (May/June 2004) and *Techniques and Technologies in Morphogenetic Design* (March/April 2006). This work was consolidated in his classic book *The Architecture of Emergence*, which in many ways provides a foundation and a preface to this current issue of ⚰, with two chapters at the end of the book dedicated to the formation and emergence of cities in the ancient world.[3]

The greatest synergies in this issue come through this focus on the material and physical sciences: whether it is SOM providing a pertinent analogy with the routine blood test and the diagnosis and intervention of the medical practitioner (see pp 86–93); Evan Greenberg and George Jeronimidis analysing the rainforest's morphology and its potential as an urban model (pp 24–31); or Groundlab on the significance of the terrain and an approach that uses ecological infrastructure as the basis for design (pp 78–85). It is also very much apparent how new technologies such as computational simulation and multi-scale analytic modelling are facilitating this approach, revealing a new sense of the city as one that is integrated into a complex network of flows and processes, and as much about physical as cultural properties.

Running counter to the main theme of the issue is Colin Fournier's energetic Counterpoint that seeks us to question any assumptions about complexity and its relationship to urban social behaviour and the system city analogy. Just how system-oriented do we want our developing perceptions of the city to be? ⚰

Notes
1. Saskia Sassen, *The Global City: New York, London, Tokyo*, Princeton University Press (Princeton, NJ), 1991.
2. Grahame Shane explains that Peter Hall credited Janice Perlman with the invention of the term 'megacity' in her PhD studies of Rio favelas in the early 1970s (published 1976). See David Grahame Shane, *Urban Design Since 1945: A Global Perspective*, John Wiley & Sons (Chichester), 2011, p 29.
3. Michael Weinstock, *The Architecture of Emergence: The Evolution of Form in Nature and Civilisation*, John Wiley & Sons (Chichester), 2010; see Chapter 7 'City Forms' and Chapter 8 'The Forms of Information, Energy and Ecology', pp 176–243.

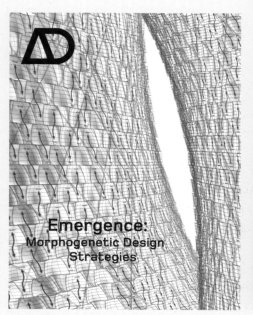

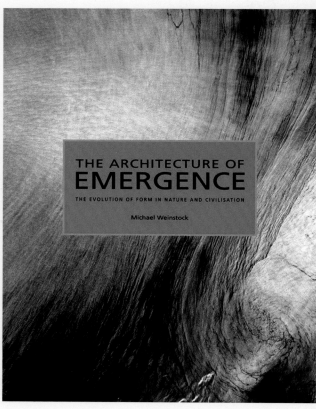

Metabolism and Morphology

Architecture is on the cusp of systemic change, driven by the dynamics of climate and economy, of new technologies and new means of production. There is a growing interest in the dynamics of fluidity, in networks and in the new topologies of surfaces and soft boundaries. This is part of a general cultural response to the contemporary reconfiguration of the concept of 'nature' within the discourse of architecture; a change from metaphor to model, from 'nature' as a source of formal inspiration to 'nature' as a mine of interrelated dynamic processes that are available for analysis and digital simulation. Michael Weinstock presents an account of the dynamics of natural metabolisms, and suggests an agenda for the development of metabolic morphologies of buildings and cities.

Form has been a central focus in the theories and practice of architecture throughout history, and over time has been aligned with many different ideologies and methods of generating the shape of buildings. The design of surfaces that capture or modify light, the design of heat-generation and transportation systems, and of systems for the movement of air are applied to forms that have been designed according to other criteria. In built architecture, morphology is prior to and separate from metabolism. In city morphologies, the designation of parks and other spaces as the 'lungs' of cities is an inexact metaphor – and a metaphor chosen from the wrong metabolism.

In the natural world, form and metabolism have a very different relationship. There is an intricate choreography of energy and material that determines the morphology of living forms, their relations to each other, and which drives the self-organisation of populations and ecological systems.

In the natural world, form and metabolism have a very different relationship. There is an intricate choreography of energy and material that determines the morphology of living forms, their relations to each other, and which drives the self-organisation of populations and ecological systems.

All living forms must acquire energy and materials from their environment, and transform this matter and energy within their bodies to construct their tissues, to grow, to reproduce and to survive. D'Arcy Wentworth Thompson argued in *On Growth and Form* that the morphology of living forms has a 'dynamical aspect, under which we deal with the interpretation, in terms of force, of the operations of Energy.' Living forms are able to construct and dynamically maintain themselves by the exchange of energy and material through their surfaces, and in doing so excrete changed materials and energy back into the environment. Morphology and metabolism are intricately linked through the processing of energy and materials. Metabolism is the fire of life,[?] and occurs at all levels from the molecular to the intricate dynamics of ecological

Theoretical optimal ratios of branch lengths produce the most equitable distribution of leaf clusters in computed branch systems, and are similar to the observed ratios in real trees.

systems. There are common metabolic characteristics for whole forms, in the relations between the geometry and overall size of the body plan, the internal operating temperature and the mode of existence in the environment.

Performance has been a central concern of discourses on contemporary architecture, and it is clear that architects today are increasingly becoming engaged with the natural world. There is a new sensitivity to the 'life' of buildings, and an understanding that performance and behaviour can be inputs to the process of design rather than functions applied later to a form. The study of natural metabolisms is a significant resource for design as it reveals that shape or morphology is deeply integrated within the means of capturing and transmitting energy. The organisation and morphology of energy systems of the natural world provide a set of models for what will become the new 'metabolic morphologies' of future buildings, and ultimately of cities.

Metabolism determines the relations of individuals and populations of natural forms with their local environment. Higher levels of biological organisation emerge from metabolic processes, in the relations between species, and in the density and patterns of distribution of species across the surface of the earth. All metabolic processes stem from the sunlight that falls on the surface of the earth. A very small percentage, perhaps less than 2 per cent, of that light energy

Branching system, leafless tree in winter. In the anatomical organisation of trees, the transportation network for fluids and the structural support for the leaf array have evolved as a fully integrated morphology. Branch angles and the ratios of length in sequential 'mother to daughter' branches determine the effective leaf area and constrain the overall morphology of a tree. They are also intrinsic characteristics of a species, so that different angles and ratios appear in different species.

Michael Weinstock is an architect, and currently Director of Research and Development, and Director of the Emergent Technologies and Design (EmTech) programme in the Graduate School of the Architectural Association (AA) School of Architecture in London. Born in Germany, he lived as a child in the Far East and then West Africa, and attended an English public school. He ran away to sea at the age of 17 after reading Conrad. After many years at sea, in traditional wooden sailing ships where he gained shipyard and shipbuilding experience, he studied architecture at the AA and has taught at its School of Architecture since 1989 in a range of positions from workshop tutor to Intermediate and then Diploma Unit Master, Master of Technical Studies and Academic Head.

Over the last decade his published work has arisen from research into the dynamics, forms and energy transactions of natural systems, and the application of the mathematics and processes of emergence to cities, groups of buildings within cities, and individual buildings. While his principal research and teaching has been conducted at the AA, he has published and lectured widely, and taught seminar courses, studios and workshops on these topics at many other schools of architecture in Europe and the US. He has made a significant contribution to the theoretical discourses of architecture, to the pedagogies of the discipline, and on practice. He has been a leader in bringing awareness and understanding of natural systems and the historical and current impacts of complexity, climatic and ecological changes on human architectures at all scales, and of the natural and human dynamics that are currently driving changes in all the systems of nature and civilisation.

He is the author of the book *The Architecture of Emergence: The Evolution of Form in Nature and Civilisation* (John Wiley & Sons, 2010), and over the years has contributed many articles to △. He also guest-edited (with Michael Hensel and Achim Menges) two previous issues of △: *Emergence: Morphogenetic Design Strategies* (May/June 2004) and *Techniques and Technologies in Morphogenetic Design* (March/April 2006). △

AMID.cero9

The Magic Mountain, Ames, Iowa, 2002
A former power station is wrapped in an ecosystem mask that converts energy infrastructures and architecture into a living system to be inserted within the city. The membrane attracts the most important butterfly and bird species in the northern US like a real mountain, and the building is converted into the laboratory of a genetic engineer, where different species and varieties of roses can be researched and developed, challenging the common tools and concepts of architecture, gardening, species breeding and the ecology of living.

AMID.cero9 with José Quintanar and Colectivo Cuartoymitad

The Big Mech and Co: Gran Vía Toxic, Madrid, 2008–10
This social engineering of a clinical order can be read as a brutal example of the 'creative destruction' concept developed by the economist Joseph Alois Schumpeter in his book *Capitalism, Socialism and Democracy* (1942). According to his thesis, modernity is an eminently creative destructive process supported by a constant succession of innovations. Drawing by Ja Ja Ja.

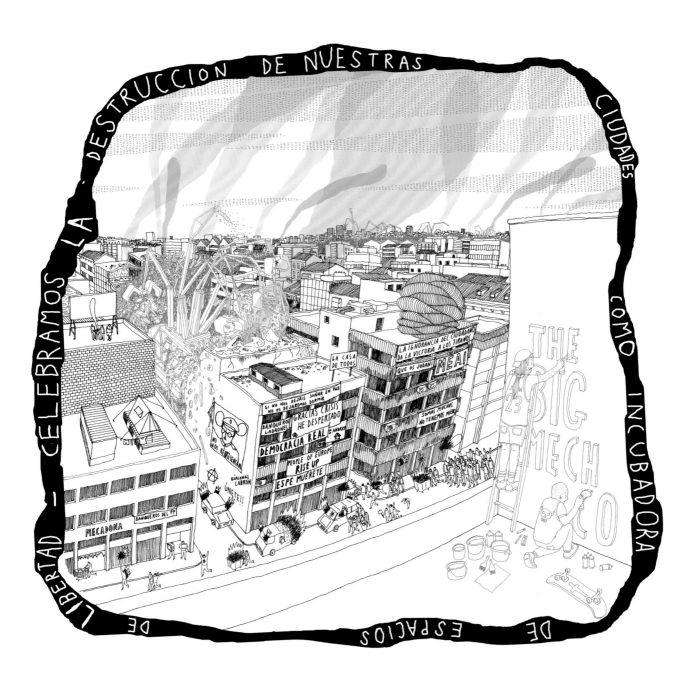

**Aedas with AECOM and
Buro Happold**

**XRL West Kowloon Terminus, Hong Kong,
due for completion 2014**
The new terminus of the Guangzhou-Shenzhen-
Hong Kong Express Rail Link (XRL) is based
on parkland that stretches over the roof
of the station, creating an informal set of
connections as well as a holding space for
waiting, lingering and social interaction.

**Cino Zucchi Architects
and One Works with
Buro Happold**

Keski-Pasila Masterplan, Helsinki, 2007
Public spaces are determined by pedestrian
and cycle paths that are embedded in the
communal usages and allow the emergence
of a secondary network and connections
over time.

Daniel Segraves

Urban Energy Data Model, Chicago Loop, 2011
The overall carbon impact attributed to each building relative to its size, shown here in red to represent heavier impact, was calculated using historic and predicted energy use, as well as many externalities such as the flow of goods and people to and from each building.

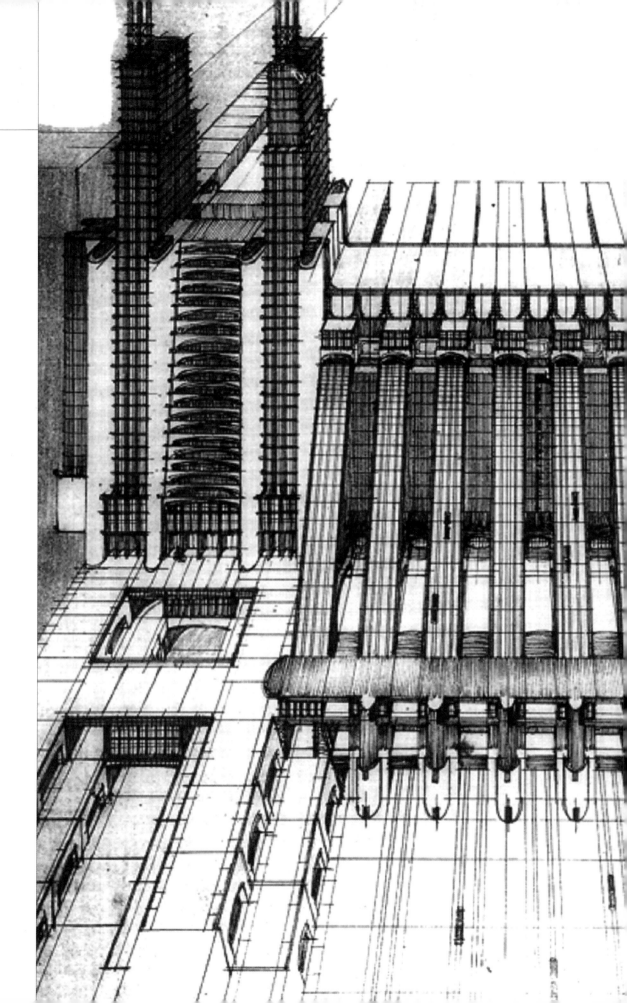

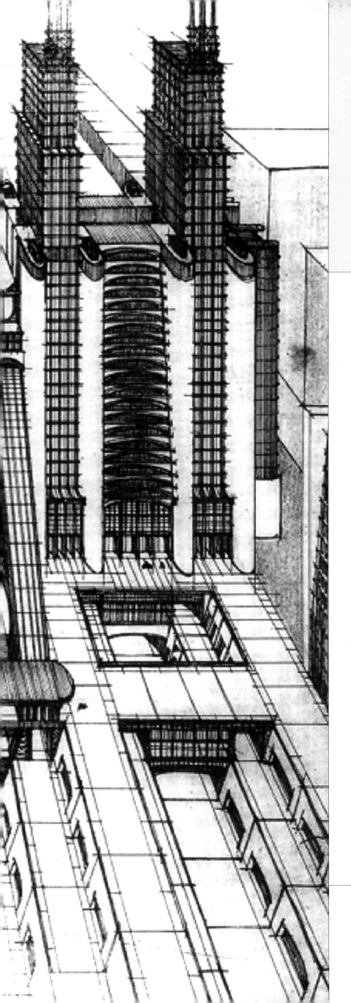

SYSTEM CITY

INFRA-STRUCTURE AND THE SPACE OF FLOWS

Antonio Sant'Elia, *La Città Nuova*, 1914
Sant'Elia's imagination of the future city was characterised
by an architecture of calculation, constructed with all the
resources of science and technological systems to satisfy
'all the demands of our habits and spirit'.

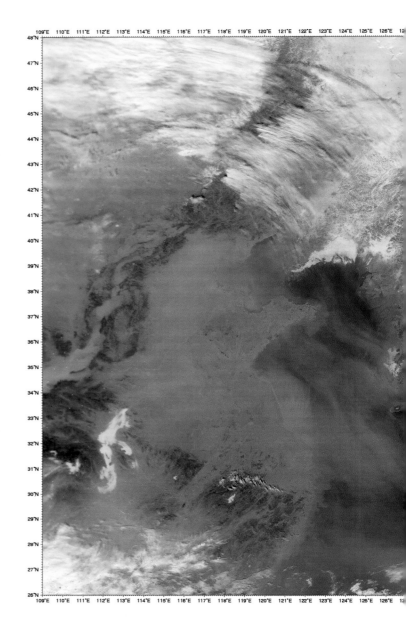

A century has passed since these words were written, and much has changed in the world. For Sant'Elia, as for architects today, the future city was a project of the imagination as much as it was of calculation, and his descriptions of a dynamic city constantly being reinvented and rebuilt, of rapid movement and change, and new ways of being, resonates most strongly today. The city is 'both real and imaginary, something lived and something dreamed, the most complex artefact of human civilisation, an object of nature and a subject of culture'.[2] It is our culture that determines the way we think about the city, and mediates our experience of it. New ways of thinking about the city and new methods of design and making it are once again emerging, engaging both the means and the imagination of our culture. *System City* brings together scientists, architects and engineers from disparate fields whose work and thoughts converge on contributing to the societal endeavour of building the 'future city'.

The need for new imaginations and new configurations of the city is more pressing now than at any previous time in human history. Two major phenomena are driving changes in the geographical distribution of populations: the migration to cities from dispersed territories, and the rapid acceleration in the growth of the number of people in the world. Migration to the city was a gradual historical phenomenon in Europe and North America, but is now a much more rapid process underway in Africa, South America and Asia. Population growth follows the same geographical distribution, being slow in the West and much faster in Africa and Asia. The centuries-long evolutionary processes that took place in the West have taken only two or three decades in Africa and Asia, and will continue to accelerate in these regions.[3]

The world is also currently in a regime of rapid climatic and ecological change, and there is widespread concern regarding the ability of the global system to cope with the array of changes that are underway or anticipated.[4] It is clear that the accelerating informational complexity, extreme velocity and volumes of fuel and food energy flowing immense distances across continents and oceans, and high but inequitable energy and material consumption[5] strongly correspond to the multiple causality of disruption, societal transformation and collapse of the past.[6] The city is critical to the capacity of society to adapt to a future of uncertainty and change.

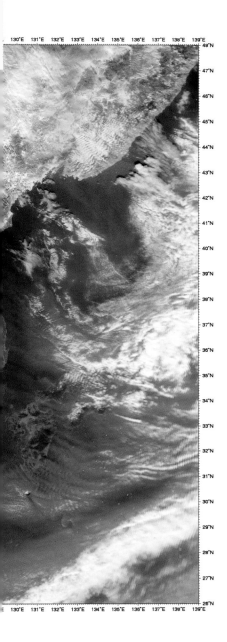

Climate, Ecology and the City

Considering the city as a dynamic complex system places emphasis on the interactions and connectivity of the flows through its infrastructures, and of the feedbacks and critical thresholds that drive the emergence of new spaces and urban morphologies that are animated by new modalities of culture. Complex systems are composed of elements that are interconnected, and causation is iterative so what is an effect at one scale may also be a cause at a higher scale.[7] In this domain cities are regarded as emergent phenomena that exhibit characteristics of complex systems, are embedded within the systems of the climate and ecology, and have reciprocal interactions between them at a variety of spatial, temporal and organisational scales.

In 'Local Climates of the City' (pp 100–105), Iain D Stewart examines how regional-scale climate produces effects on the thermal and morphological properties of urban and rural surfaces. Urban climate phenomena exist across a continuum of scales that connect the city surface and its roughness elements to the enveloping atmosphere, driven by inputs, throughputs and outputs of energy, and set out a new classification of urban microclimates. Regional-scale climates also affect the flow of energy through the ecological system of the rainforest. Evan Greenberg and George Jeronimidis' 'Variation and Distribution: Forest Patterns as a Model for Urban Morphologies' (pp 24–31) analyses the rainforest's morphology, and traces how it emerges from the interaction of climate with the flows of energy and genetic information through its individuals. The distribution patterns and growth strategies produce sectional differentiation in the forest and its microclimates, and this provides a conceptual model for the generation of urban forms organised by patterns of distribution, local height differentiations and density gradients. In turn, stratified urban microclimates are produced that can be linked to the network of green spaces and productive surfaces at the ground level.

Wax Market, Lagos, Nigeria
left: While population growth and the development of the city networks of the West evolved over a period of centuries, cities in Africa and Asia are under immense pressure to adapt to the rapid rates of population growth over only two or three decades.

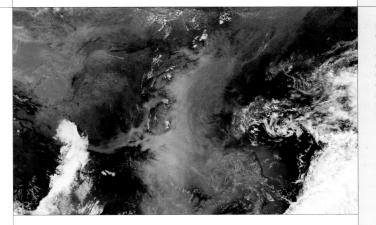

Satellite images of smog and dust clouds over China
top and left: The city is a dynamic and complex system embedded within environmental flows across a variety of scales. Smog and dust systems, for example, emerge from the combined processes of the productions of cities and conurbations and creating regional-scale climate phenomena.

In 'Scales of Metabolic Flows' (pp 86–93), Keith Besserud, Mark Sarkisian, Phil Enquist and Craig Hartman of Skidmore, Owings & Merrill (SOM) elucidate how the understanding of the differing scales and metrics of metabolic flows through cities drives their analytical and design processes. At the regional scale, the SOM study of hydrological and ecological complexities informs their 100-year vision for the Great Lakes and St Lawrence River region. The large urban project in Chicago on the Lake Michigan shoreline is integrated with the existing systems of the mature city, and emphasises the necessity for multi-scalar connectivity of hydrological and movement systems. Their urban information model of the city of San Francisco has been developed to collate the data of these flows in relation to the morphology of the city.

Daniel Segraves has also worked on the problems of collating the 'big data' of energy flows through the centre of Chicago, and in 'Data City: Urban Metabolic Decision Processes' (pp 120–23) proposes that a working model of the city will consist of numeric representations of all the flows and physical compositions of its parts in the context of the atmospheric conditions and fluctuations. Such a complete set of data would require the development of a regional-scale sensory system. The manipulation of these data during the process of city design is addressed in 'Ex Silico Ad Vivo' (pp 106–11) in which Francis Aish, Adam Davis and Martha Tsigkari of Foster + Partners explain how the existing competencies of analysis and modelling of urban environmental flows can be augmented by 'population thinking'. In this approach, a family of design options is produced, sharing genes of expressed parameterised variation that enable the evolution 'in silico' of systems via simulation processes that can also incorporate intuition and experience.

The integration of ecological, hydrological and city systems are the design drivers for new urban morphologies in the work of Eva Castro, José Alfredo Ramírez and Eduardo Rico at Groundlab. In 'The Grounds of a Renewed Practice' (pp 78–85) they present the manifestation of this approach in Ground Ecologies, a masterplan proposal for 200,000 inhabitants in the Jiading District of Shanghai. In their Paisajes Latentes project the analysis of the hydrological systems of Mexico City are coupled to the topology of Valle de Chalco's street networks to produce a synthesis of landscape infrastructure and architecture, developing new spatial patterns and adjacencies.

Cultural Systems

As humans are incorporated within the complex system, there is an increasing area of studies of the cultural aspects of the complex systems of cities. Over the last decades, the study of the city as a complex system has grown from a little-known specialised field of physics to an established and widespread collaborative research that crosses disciplinary and domain boundaries in the sciences and humanities. Culture is the collective memory of society; it encodes ways of being and the means by which each generation is bound into society and through which they contribute to it. Cultural systems are embedded in the intricate choreography of the evolution of cities and inflect their evolutionary dynamic.

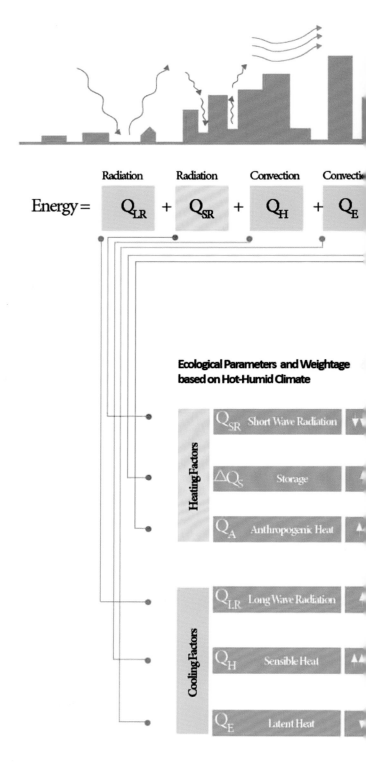

$$\text{Energy} = Q_{LR} + Q_{SR} + Q_H + Q_E$$

Radiation — Radiation — Convection — Convection

Ecological Parameters and Weightage based on Hot-Humid Climate

Heating Factors

Q_{SR} Short Wave Radiation

$\triangle Q_S$ Storage

Q_A Anthropogenic Heat

Cooling Factors

Q_{LR} Long Wave Radiation

Q_H Sensible Heat

Q_E Latent Heat

...duction   Conduction   Human
            (rural)

$$Q_S + Q_G + Q_A$$

...rphological Indicators   **Weightage for Design Criteria**

++ +
+++

- - -
++ +

+++

++ +

- --

+++
+++

+++

+++

Sebastiaan Leenknegt, Lei Liu and Aarathi Muralidharan, Ecological Parameters Affecting the Environmental Performance of the City, AA Emergent Technologies and Design (EmTech), Architectural Association, London, 2011–13
Simulations of the environmental performance of urban morphology have to encompass a series of intricate interactions of several parameters. Differential weighting of these parameters is dependent on cultural and social values.

Marina Lathouri's 'A History of Territories, Movements and Borders: Politics of Inhabitation' (pp 32–7) explores the relationship between people and territory, expanding from the scale of the intimate to the scale of geography. In her account, borders are the interfaces between the private and the public, the individual and the collective. This is also where new cultural practices play out the articulation of indeterminacy, and where the spaces of the social are created and defined. The construction of social spaces is the critical concern of Cristina Díaz Moreno and Efrén García Grinda of AMID.cero9. In 'Third Natures: Incubators of Public Space' (pp 46–55) they argue that public space is not just defined by the buildings that enclose it, but also by the interactions of people and technology as they inhabit space. What they describe as 'third natures' are self-assembled communities that construct social space through their cultural practices. In Jack Self's view, the city is a multiplex superposition of evolved network infrastructures whose origins may be traced far back in the distant past. In 'Darwin Among the Machines' (pp 66–71) he argues that contemporary informational technologies augment the social practices of the city's inhabitants, and free them to engage with public space in new and often startling ways.

Cultural evolution is intertwined with genetic evolution,[8] but neither can be neatly mapped onto the other. Humans became behaviourally modern when they could reliably transmit accumulated informational capital to the next generation, and do so with sufficient precision for knowledge to be preserved and accumulated. However, there are many differences between the evolutionary processes of culture and nature. The pace of cultural evolution is quite different to that of biological evolution, as the paths and modes of information transfer in culture are more frequent and have a far more rapid proliferation through populations than genetic transfers of information from one generation to the next. What is common between them is that both are situated, so that when changes occur in the collective behaviour of humans it tends to bring about changes in the environment, and that in turn has set up changes in the regime of natural selection.

Cultural evolution is intertwined with genetic evolution, but neither can be neatly mapped onto the other.

Integration Impact

0   1

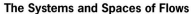

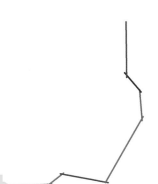

The Systems and Spaces of Flows

'Infrastructure' is the collective term for the systems and spaces of flows[9] that provide the 'services' of the city; its transportation, water, energy, information and communications, waste collection and disposal, public spaces including the 'green' spaces of parks, gardens, open woodlands or nature reserves, and the social programmes of health, education and recreation. The study and design of infrastructures is conventionally focused on the separate physical artefacts of the networks, and in recent times there has been strong focus on the architectural renewal of stations, bridges and terminals, but less on how infrastructural systems interact with their local tissues.

Wolf Mangelsdorf's 'Metasystems of Urban Flow' (pp 94–9) comments on a recent shift in the design of urban infrastructures that is based on the recognition of how multi-scalar patterns and variable speed of flows can produce emergent spatial configurations. He presents an argument for flow systems that have a measure of indeterminacy in their relations to immediate context to allow sufficient flexibility for future change. Buro Happold's approach is demonstrated in the High Line in New York City, where the reworking of the old railway infrastructure has acted as a catalyst for urban regeneration along its path. In the XRL terminus in West Kowloon the flows are more constant, but the building itself provides the gradation of spaces and programmes that mediates the transition from high-speed train to pedestrian flow into the new waterfront developments of the West Kowloon Cultural District.

In 'Cities and Grids: In Search of New Paradigms' (pp 72–7), Joan Busquets shows a taxonomy of the distinct variations of grid system street patterns of cities, each producing different spatial orders and widely distributed across historical time and geographical distance. He argues that though grid systems produce urban coherence, they have also enabled adaptations to new city functions that emerge as urban societies have evolved. He suggests a new paradigm is emerging in contemporary urban projects, a multilayered three-dimensional grid system differentiated at territorial, urban and finer-capillary scales.

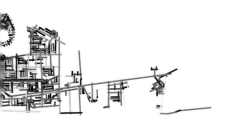

Javier Cardós Elena, Dennis Goff and Mary Polites, Adaptation of the Transportation Network of Lagos, Nigeria, AA Emergent Technologies and Design (EmTech), Architectural Association, London, 2011–13
The existing infrastructural networks within the city are highly stressed and must be adapted for rapid acceleration in population growth.

The topology and dynamics of network systems is a major area of research in complexity studies, but as yet is rarely focused on the interdependencies between differing infrastructural systems and their potential integration. However, it is now clear that developing strategies for the adaptation of existing city systems, and the design of new systems adapted to the accelerating changes of climate and population, requires integrated system analysis. Infrastructural networks do exhibit some characteristics that appear to be similar to those exhibited by the branching metabolic networks of living forms, of which the most frequently studied is the 'scale-free' power law ubiquitous in nature. Power laws describe empirical scaling relationships that are emergent quantitative features of the underlying physics of biological processes, and so are also applicable to artificially constructed network systems. Sergi Valverde and Ricard V Solé in 'Networks and the City' (pp 112–19) show that the reason that many biological and artificial networks share common features is because they operate under similar constraints, including spatial embedding, optimisation and self-organisation. The streets of the city are organised into networks, and buildings are themselves reticulated networks embedded in other networks that sustain our lives in the city.

It is thought that biological and artificial networks both grow by the addition of new nodes or hubs, and that these tend to preferentially attach to nodes that are already well connected. Flow patterns are dominated by the highly connected nodes, through which flows the maximum volume and velocity of energy, information or material. This preferential connectivity makes the networks robust as the greater majority of nodes have few links, so a random failure of any one node will only affect a local area of the network. However, if a node with a high number of connections fails, the scale-free characteristics of the entire network will be affected, and it may fail altogether.[10] The scaling patterns in city infrastructures and their relation to the periodicities, velocities and quantities of flows through their systems are related to the size of city, and the larger the city the faster all of its processes are. This has effects on the pace of life and has led to shortening cycles between major urban reconfigurations and renewals, now estimated to be shorter than a human lifetime.[11]

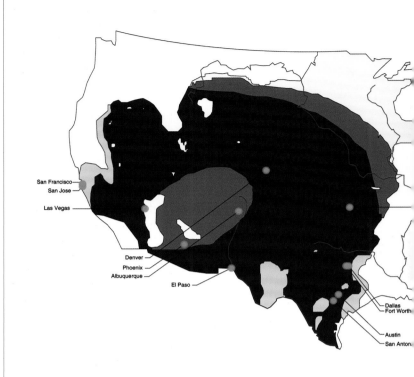

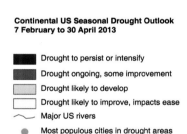

**Continental US Seasonal Drought Outlook
7 February to 30 April 2013**

- Drought to persist or intensify
- Drought ongoing, some improvement
- Drought likely to develop
- Drought likely to improve, impacts ease
- Major US rivers
- Most populous cities in drought areas

Mehran Gharleghi, Model of the City, AA Emergent Technologies and Design (EmTech), Architectural Association, 2013–14
right: The morphological model of differentiated gradients and densities is connected to numerical models of network infrastructures and their dynamic flows, and to mathematical evaluation of environmental performance to test adaptive reconfigurations under development.

Major US cities by population located within projected drought areas, 7 February to 30 April 2013
All major city systems within the zone, and the continental-scale water distribution network, are in need of development and adaptation strategies to cope with changes in local and regional climatic conditions.

Imagining and building the future city is central to the future of humans

Society has already begun to transit through the long-anticipated threshold of an explosion in 'information' and associated new technologies, and the social and economic consequences have made substantial transformations of cities. Public and social space were once strongly linked to the traditional neighbourhood of the historical city, in which 'local' was a bounded space, defined by proximity – what is 'local' is more difficult to define today. We are more mobile, and our social and work relations are spread over a larger area than in the past. There is, in consequence, an emergent sense of locality as something more personally constructed, a patchwork of people and places united not by proximity, but by our ability to move between them. They are assembled into coherent wholes by our physical and digital journeys, and it is these journeys that constitute the network of connections that animate our individual lives and synthesise societal dynamics with the spaces of the city. Liam Young and Kate Davies explore and document the emerging landscapes from which the materials that support the mechanisms of contemporary life are extracted and which flow across the earth. 'A Distributed Ground: The Unknown Fields Division' (pp 38–45) presents a narrative account of a speculative supply chain that begins 1 kilometre (0.6 miles) below the surface of the Western Desert in outback Australia, continues to the Arctic 'Northwest Passage' and on to London. It is a dialogue between the immediate and the remote, a means of conveying the logistics, trajectories and distributed territories of the contemporary and future city.

The Future City

Imagining and building the future city is central to the future of humans in the regime of rapidly accelerating population growth and declining resources, climatic and ecological change, and accelerating complexity of the global system. In 'Intelligent Cities and the Taxonomy of Cognitive Scales' (pp 56–65) I have set out, with the help of Mehran Gharleghi, an outline of the specifics of the intelligence required for integration of sentient urban infrastructural systems into an intelligent 'metasystem' that is sensitively coupled to the lives of its citizens. It is a preliminary conceptual schema of cognitive categories in ascending order of complexity: the 'situated city', 'reactive/responsive city', 'adaptive/attentional city' and the 'self-aware city'. The future city is fully intelligent. It is self-aware and 'conscious' of both itself and its citizens, and able to synchronise the city systems with climatic and ecological phenomena at the regional and local scales. Its spatial patterns are culturally appropriate to its citizens, and it adapts itself to the fluctuations of its flows, and to the emergent phenomena of its cultural practices by expansions, contractions and reconfigurations of its infrastructural systems, its spatial patterns and the morphology of its architecture. ⚙

Notes
1. Antonio Sant'Elia, 'Manifesto of Futurist Architecture', in 'Messaggio', the foreword in the catalogue of the 'Città Nuova' exhibition, Milan, 1914 (thought to be later appropriated and edited by Filippo Marinetti).
2. Claude Lévi-Strauss, *Tristes Tropiques*, Librairie Plon (Paris), 1955, trans John Weightman and Doreen Weightman, Jonathan Cape (London), 1973, p 155.
3. World population is projected to be over 9 billion by 2050. From the 2010 Revision of the World Population Prospects, Population Division of the United Nations Department of Economic and Social Affairs of the United Nations Secretariat.
4. Paul Ehrlich and Anne Ehrlich, 'Can a Collapse of Global Civilization be Avoided?', *Philosophical Transactions of the Royal Society of London* B 280, 2013.
5. Karl Butzer and Georgina Enfield, 'Critical Perspectives on Historical Collapse', *Proceedings of the National Academy of Sciences*, Vol 109, No 10, 2012, pp 3628–31.
6. Michael Weinstock, *The Architecture of Emergence: The Evolution of Form in Nature and Civilisation*, John Wiley & Sons (Chichester), 2010, pp 261-9.
7. Peter A Corning, 'The Re-Emergence of "Emergence": A Venerable Concept in Search of a Theory', *Complexity* 7 (6), 2002, pp 18–30.
8. Herbert Gintis, 'Gene-Culture Coevolution and the Nature of Human Sociality', *Philosophical Transactions of the Royal Society of London* B 366(1566), 2011, pp 878–88.
9. The phrase 'space of flows' was first used by Manuel Castells to describe the effect of information networks as transforming society, a change from 'spaces of place' to the 'space of flows'. Manuel Castells, *The Informational City: Information Technology, Economic Restructuring, and the Urban Regional Process*, Basil Blackwell (London), 1989, p 146.
10. Ricard V Solé and José M Montoya, 'Complexity and Fragility in Ecological Networks', *Proceedings of the Royal Society* B 268, 2001, pp 2039–45, and Marti Rosas-Casals, Sergi Valverde and Ricard V Solé, 'Topological Vulnerability of the European Power Grid Under Errors and Attacks', International Journal of Bifurcation and Chaos, 2007, pp 2465–75.
11. Luís MA Bettencourt, José Lobo and Geoffrey B West, 'Why are Large Cities Faster? Universal Scaling and Self-Similarity in Urban Organization and Dynamics', *European Physical Journal* B 63, 2008, pp 285–93.

Evan Greenberg and George Jeronimidis

FOREST PATTERNS AS A MODEL FOR URBAN MORPHOLOGIES

VARIATION AND DISTRIBUTION

The distribution patterns of trees in the rainforest have developed over thousands of years through cycles of growth and decay, competition and adaptation. Emerging from this dynamic yet homeostatic process, that is, one capable of internal regulation to maintain a state of equilibrium, is a complex global morphology with differentiated microclimates, generated from a finely tuned coordination of flows of various information and energy networks. This spatial logic can be extracted and developed as a new model for city systems, where the distribution of morphological variation at ground level coupled with sectional height differentiation generate productive microclimates capable of environmental negotiation and dynamic spatial and cultural effects.

British biologist D'Arcy Wentworth Thompson states in his seminal work *On Growth and Form* (1915) that 'the form of an object is a "diagram of forces", in this sense, at least, that from it we can judge of or deduce the forces that are acting or have acted upon it'.[1] In biology, all living forms obtain a specific morphology through the collection, negotiation and exchange of energy. This metabolic process is crucial in the development of individual forms, and even more so in the relationship between individuals.[2] The flow of energy and information between individuals creates emergent patterns within the collective, with higher levels of functionality and performance. This association has been well researched in social insects such as termites, ants and bees, where each individual is programmed with a specific set of tasks and interactions, creating highly specialised morphologies with precisely controlled microclimates. Forests are collectives of trees competing for resources and coordinating energy exchange. The morphological outcome of these relations is a highly diverse forest, especially in tropical climates, capable of providing a suitable environment for a vast number of plant and animal species within differentiated productive microclimates.

What can we learn from the spatial logic of collections of trees in the rainforest? **Evan Greenberg** of the EmTech programme at the Architectural Association (AA) School of Architecture in London and **George Jeronimidis** of the Centre for Biomimetics at the University of Reading combine forces to analyse the rainforest's morphology and its potential as an urban model. They suggest how the sectional height differentiation of trees could present a new way of thinking about urban organisation, accommodating varied microclimates, programmes and the city's infrastructural flows.

The forest is a highly complex and diversified environment, covering roughly 30 per cent of the earth's land mass.[3] The first forests emerged 360 million years ago through the evolution of water algae and primitive plants in response to continental drift and carbon dioxide availability. By responding to the need for stronger root systems, maximum exposure to sunlight and land reproduction strategies, these organisms evolved into larger plants with advanced vascular systems, roots and leaves, eventually becoming the first trees.[4] Trees evolved in groups, as forest patches, yet individually as singular species, creating layered 'forest communities'.[5] The earliest trees, and specifically seed-producing trees, evolved the ability to reproduce globally over vast land areas, and in time, competition among trees gave way to deeper roots, differential branching strategies, complex flow structures and intelligent leaf organisations.[6] All trees share these characteristics, and all species follow particular mathematical models for growth, adaptation and survival. Within these models, each species follows a predefined genetic rule set modulated by adaptations to environmental pressures while still allowing for response to competitive pressures.

From the study of the evolution of tree populations, it is possible to relate mathematical and functional patterns of the forest to the design of cities and their networks. By understanding the initial genetic rule set of individual trees, and the relationships between the hierarchies in which they exist in the forest, intelligence can be designed into buildings and their arrangement within the city to generate highly performative urban organisations capable of negotiating environmental conditions, managing energy flows, distributing infrastructural networks and creating complex spatial and microclimatic environments.

Trees have an incredibly complex internal organisation focused on the capture and distribution of sunlight and water. They are made of cellulose fibres stiffened in tension, giving them the structural effectiveness to not only stand up, but also to create transportation networks for the flow of water from roots to leaves, and energy captured from leaves to roots. The mathematical branching and leaf arrangement logics present in trees optimise structure and the transfer of materials within.[7] In isolation, a tree will grow with a straight vertical trunk and branch patterns designed to maximise canopy exposure to the sun at specific latitudes.[8] But however calculated the material organisation and mathematical logics of trees may be, they rarely conform to their optimality model, and are in a constant state of morphogenesis. Trees grow in response primarily to gravity and sunlight, and develop specialised tissues, tension and compression wood – depending on species – in order to support unexpected directional growth of branches and achieve shape adaptation of trunks.

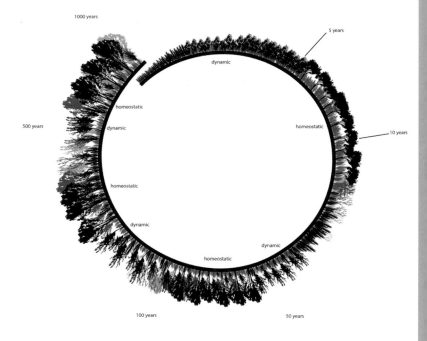

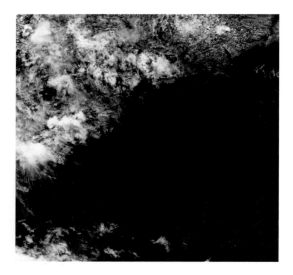

Overhead view of the Amazon rainforest
Thirty per cent of the earth's land mass is covered by forests, home to thousands of diverse species living in differentiated ecosystems and microclimates throughout the world. Geneticist and evolutionary biologist Theodosius Dobzhansky concluded in 1950 that the increase in biological diversity from the poles to the equator was a result of multiple small but stable forest habitats.

Phases of sylvigenesis in a tropical rainforest
above: The rainforest is in a constant flux of growth and decay. Its sylvigenesis is a homeostatic process of negotiating numerous flows of energy.

Structural ensembles of a tropical rainforest
opposite: The rainforest is a series of dense layers comprised of three major structural ensembles: trees of the past, present and future.

Similar patterns of growth can be observed when looking at a collection of trees in the forest, and more specifically in the rainforest. The constant sylvigenesis, or generation of the forest's global form, is a homeostatic process, distributing various flows of energy within a constant state of equilibrium. While the energy captured by individual trees cannot be redistributed directly to surrounding individuals, there exist explicit interactions between forest hierarchies and individual organisms in relation to energy consumption, employment of resources, recycling of materials and spatial organisations.[9] The competition for light resources, in fact, is believed to have led to the synthesis of the natural adhesive lignin[10] in trees, which is produced within the cell walls and responsible for binding the cellulose fibres together. This allows trees to be structurally stiff, and hence to grow taller and increase canopy size giving them the ability to survive as energy-capturing and energy-distributing organisms.

Competition not only affects morphogenesis of the single organism, but also of the entire forest. Rather than the common view of the existence of four global strata (emergents, canopy, understorey and forest floor), the rainforest can be seen as a series of layers of varying densities, or 'structural ensembles', comprising individuals with three morphogenetic strategies. The first group require no further growth, in that their crowns are exposed to the sunlight necessary for maximum energy capture and conversion, and they have achieved their genetic limit. The second group are typically in the forest understories, and are either expanding or waiting to expand – they will very rapidly fill any 'light niche' that becomes available when a large tree falls down. Finally, there are also damaged or dead trees that do not compete actively as do the other groups, but slow down the growth of neighbouring trees.[11]

As the rainforest is destroyed by wind, earthquakes, animals or other natural phenomena, branches or entire trees fall to the forest floor, damaging some trees below, but also allowing for trees in lower structural ensembles to take advantage and grow into the gaps that result.[12] The first structural ensemble possesses the densest canopy and limits solar access to the ground. While it is true that all trees require sunlight to grow and multiply, the trees in the second structural ensemble survive through the adaptation of chlorophyll distribution and the maximisation of the photosynthesis process. Trees in these underlayers tend to have larger leaves of a darker green or blue colour to make greatest use of the available sunlight. Additionally, some leaves contain red hues that scatter light through the tree canopy, and velvety or satin textures that focus light down towards the forest floor.[13] From a larger ecosystemic view, the effects of the dense canopy on the rainforest create completely new microclimates which are both comfortable and highly productive for many other trees and plants, fruits, insects, birds and other animals.[14] In fact, these conditions are essential in the sylvigenesis of the rainforest through the symbiotic relationships that exist between various species.

But however calculated
the material organisation
and mathematical logics
of trees may be, they
rarely conform to their
optimality model,
and are in a constant
state of morphogenesis.

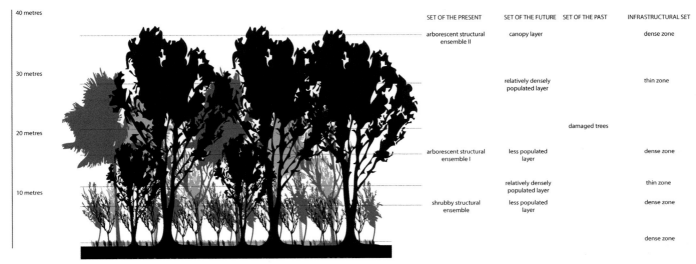

While many forests, particularly in continental and colder climates, contain little variation among species, within the sectional layers of the tropical rainforest lies an exceedingly differentiated population, where often only one individual per species per hectare exists.[15] This hierarchical relationship between global structural ensembles and local diversity is especially evident in rainforests[16] and allows for clever adaptation and extreme robustness under varying conditions. Forest gaps provide intense spots of sunlight exposure that in turn allow for extremely rapid growth. Additionally, the gaps create varied microclimates with differentiated lighting, moisture and wind conditions.[17] Thus the forest responds to environmental pressures at different rates. While gap dynamics and the trees that respond to them are specific to larger events that occur within the forest, all trees must also adapt to seasonal and daily climatic changes. Chemical signals are spread through the air downwind, and trees (although not as frequently as herbaceous plants)[18] can communicate with each other regarding mechanical or predatory damage. Communication also occurs chemically underground between root systems. While trees cannot uproot and move locations, they can induce structural and internal organisational changes to aid defence. The ability to communicate through environmentally distributed signals can often allow trees to expend energy for effective defensive response, reducing the number of late responses to predators and other failures.[19] In the forest, trees also use these signals to anticipate environmental patterns and shed leaves or blossom flowers accordingly in order to conserve energy resources. This response is a global coordination[20] scattered with local specialised events.

So while individual trees are programmed with specific strategies for growth and survival, the rainforest's emergent morphology is a complex result of adaptation to competition among highly differentiated individuals and a finely tuned coordination of flows of various information and energy networks. Through this understanding of the forest's spatial logic, distribution patterns and growth strategies, we can begin to develop similar systems for cities. The city has been referred to as an organism since the late 19th and early 20th centuries by urban planners such as Ebenezer Howard and Patrick Geddes, with a predefined optimal size, cohesive integrated infrastructure and inherent tendency towards homeostasis.[21] And across numerous scales of hierarchy, just like natural systems, cities too have a lifecycle of birth, growth, maturity and decay.

Due to changes at the local, regional and global scales in both human and environmental flows, the infrastructural and information networks within the city are in constant flux. Furthermore, contemporary technology allows individual buildings to communicate through intelligent building material systems embedded with sensing, management and actuation capabilities. Just as trees can react to changes within the forest, buildings can now also sense environmental conditions in real time and react through adjustments to their material makeup. These local building interactions, however, are part of the larger collective system that is the city. A building's ability to filter and modulate the environment has a larger effect on both internal and external climates and incidental effects throughout the entire city.

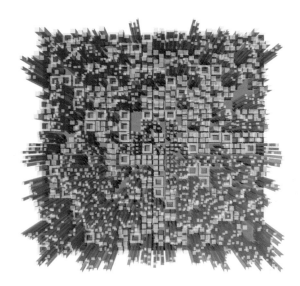

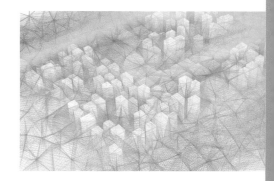

Urban patch utilising the concept of structural ensembles
above and top right: Urban blocks fit within three overlapping height bands (12–24 metres, 18–42 metres and 40–90 metres) in order to generate density differentiation while limiting repetitive block morphologies.

Differentiated air velocities due to morphological variation
bottom right: By varying the planar and sectional distribution of urban block morphologies, a large number of differentiated microclimates emerge three-dimensionally, with varied air velocities and ventilation rates.

Environmental negotiation therefore has a direct effect on morphology and the creation of productive microclimates. This urban form can arise out of the patterns of distribution of city blocks based on the logic of structural ensembles in the rainforest. The specific location of a tree species is governed predominantly by the dispersal and deposition of seeds and establishment of root systems. While these processes are not random, they are also not integral to the observed patterns of the structural ensembles, as each dense layer of the rainforest contains numerous different species acting within its stratum. The emergent effects of the forest are not therefore dependent on their planar position in the forest, but directly linked to their strata, governed by their embodied energy and past, present and future growth strategies.

By designing the city with structural ensembles in mind, city organisations can take advantage of controlled natural lighting conditions and canyon wind flow regimes. Cities are often designed in density gradients, locating specific programmatic districts, 'downtowns' and outskirts. However, by scattering densities throughout, there is the possibility to create numerous microclimates through a series of scales: from neighbourhoods and blocks to urban squares and market streets, down to bus stops and pedestrian walkways. By using a three-dimensional approach to design focused on sectional strata rather than planar zoning, buildings' blocks can be designed by height categories with varying street widths in order to control wind velocity and solar access to create differentiated microclimates at ground level. The emergence of varied solar access patterns can be coupled to patterns of airflow in order to achieve desired light and ventilation conditions. Building heights control solar access at ground level; street widths can then be optimised in order to increase or decrease natural ventilation, affecting the perceived temperatures for pedestrians. By generating sections where large building heights are coupled with narrow street widths (height-to-width ratios above 0.65), or small building heights with very wide streets (height-to-width ratios below 0.5), users at ground level are sheltered from high wind speeds, but also subjected to poor ventilation. On the other hand, designing with height-to-width ratios between 0.5 and 0.65 allows for lower wind speeds and possible natural ventilation.[22] Through a careful choreography of local height differentiations and street dimensions, desired microclimates can thus be achieved. This in turn allows for urban uses in pockets of specificity and intensity not necessarily suitable for a specific regional climate.

Canyon wind flow regimes
The height-to-width ratio of urban canyons creates changes in wind speeds at ground level while also encouraging or retarding natural ventilation. Top to bottom: An isolated roughness flow with a height-to-width ratio between 0.3 and 0.5 creates wind patterns similar to isolated buildings; a wake interference flow with a height-to-width ratio between 0.5 and 0.65 creates low wind speeds and turbulence, promoting ventilation; a skimming flow does not allow a great deal of wind to enter between buildings, resulting in poor street ventilation.

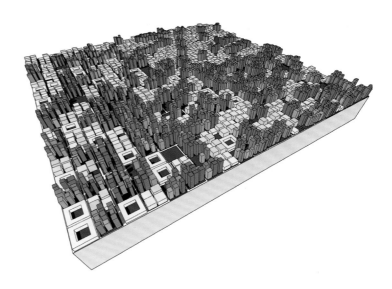

Height gradients of an urban patch
An urban morphology generated with gradients of heights and densities across blocks can create varied microclimates and unexpected yet productive urban environments.

The urban fabric is
rich and diverse,
and thus becomes
a heterogeneous
landscape of emergent
interactions within
a homeostatic
environment.

However, the application of different strata to the design of cities must not be limited to environmental effects at street level. Taller blocks, with inherently larger energy demands, have the ability to collect solar energy while providing gradients of self-shading to buildings at lower heights. This decrease of indirect light in certain climates can increase user comfort inside buildings. The availability of useable rooftops, balconies and raised transportation networks is then potentially increased. These spaces become intrinsically linked to the network of green spaces and productive surfaces located in blocks at the ground level. They can be used to generate food resources for the city's inhabitants, immediately linking the productivity of the city to its users. And just as gaps provide varied environmental conditions in the forest, so too can this network of green spaces allow for yet another type of urban microclimate: areas where sun exposure is desired, but also where transpiration occurs to cool the city. The three-dimensional distribution of green spaces throughout the city creates unique morphological relationships between buildings, blocks and transportation networks, and fosters emergent environments, microclimates and interactions that traditionally planned cities may not inherently provide.

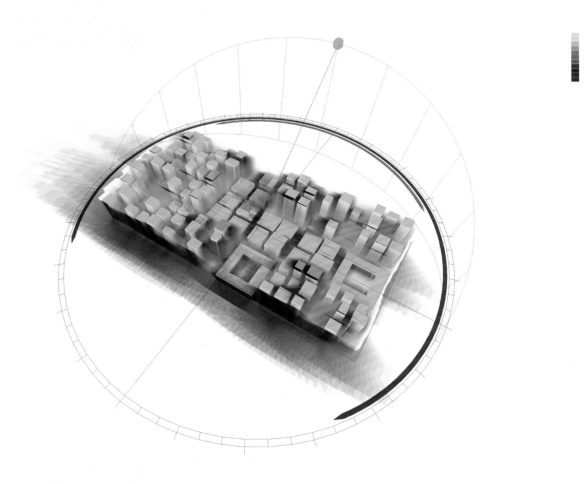

Differentiated solar radiation due to morphological variation
Varied morphological distribution throughout a city patch results in large differential gradients of solar radiation not just at ground level, but three-dimensionally throughout.

Sectional height differentiation as a design driver not only dictates formal variation, but also specific organisational effects that accommodate varied microclimates, programmes and, ultimately, infrastructural flows throughout the city. Diverse density gradients derived from varied distribution within strata create new and unexpected associations between networks, nodes and individuals. The urban fabric is rich and diverse, and thus becomes a heterogeneous landscape of emergent interactions within a homeostatic environment. Like the rainforest, the urban environment can benefit from structured differentiation in typology and form; cities equipped with varied microclimates allow for different activities with effective energy usage and information flows. In this way, the city becomes an agent in its own productivity, with the exchange of energy and information leading to the dynamic growth of urban space and culture. ∆

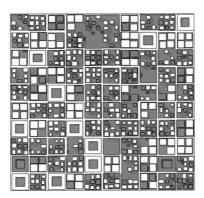

1. D'Arcy Wentworth Thompson, *On Growth and Form: The Complete Revised Edition*, Dover Publications (New York), 1992, p 16.
2. Michael Weinstock, *The Architecture of Emergence: The Evolution of Form in Nature and Civilisation*, John Wiley & Sons (Chichester), 2010, pp 119–20.
3. Based on data published in 2005 by the Food and Agriculture Organisation of the United Nations: ftp://ftp.fao.org/docrep/fao/010/i0105e/i0105e03.pdf, accessed 19 February 2013.
4. KJ Willis and JC McElwain, *The Evolution of Plants*, Oxford University Press (New York), 2002, p 86.
5. Paul Kendrick and Peter R Crane, 'The Origin and Evolution of Plants on Land', *Nature*, Vol 389, 4 Sept 1997, p 36.
6. Willis and McElwain, op cit.
7. For an in-depth observation on branching logics in trees and other natural systems, see Evan Greenberg, 'Observation, Analysis and Computation of Branching Patterns in Natural Systems', in Andrew Kudless, Neri Oxman and Marc Swackhamer (eds), *Silicon + Skin: Biological Processes and Computation, Proceedings of the 28th Annual Conference of the Association for Computer Aided Design in Architecture (ACADIA)*, Association for Computer Aided Design in Architecture, 2010, pp 316–23.
8. Francis Hallé, Roelof AA Oldeman and Philip Barry Tomlinson, *Tropical Trees and Forests: An Architectural Analysis*, Springer-Verlag (Berlin), 1978, p 278.
9. Ibid, p 372.
10. Kendrick and Crane, op cit.
11. Hallé, Oldeman and Tomlinson, op cit, pp 320–5.
12. Ibid, p 320.
13. Martin Ingrouille, *Diversity and Evolution of Land Plants*, Chapman & Hall (London), 1992, p 207.
14. Colin Tudge, *The Secret Life of Trees: How They Live and Why They Matter*, Penguin Books (London), 2006, p 295.
15. AA Federov, 'The Structure of the Tropical Rainforest and Speciation in the Humid Tropics', *Journal of Ecology*, No 54, 1996, p 4.
16. Research has shown that a 2-hectare (5-acre) patch of the Panama rainforest has two and a half times more species than the same size patch in the Vermont rainforest. For more on this subject see Robert H MacArthur, 'Patterns of Communities in the Tropics', *Biological Journal of the Linnean Society*, Vol 1, 1969, p 23.
17. John Kircher, *A Neotropical Companion: An Introduction to the Animals, Plants and Ecosystems of New World Tropics*, Princeton University Press (Princeton, NJ), 1997, pp 57–8.
18. Marcel Dicke and Jan Bruin, 'Chemical Information Transfer Between Plants: Back to the Future', *Biochemical Systematics and Ecology*, No 29, 2001, p 983.
19. Ibid.
20. Colin Tudge, op cit, pp 267, 274.
21. Spiro Kostof, *The City Shaped: Urban Patterns and Meanings Through History*, Thames & Hudson (London), 1991, pp 15–16.
22. Evyatar Erell, David Pearlmutter and Terry Williamson, *Urban Microclimate: Designing the Spaces Between Buildings*, Earthscan (London), 2011, pp 88–9.

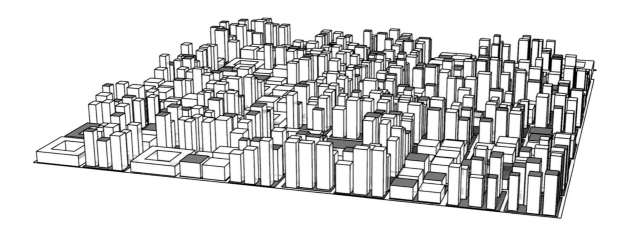

Distribution network of urban green spaces
The distribution of differentiated blocks throughout the city creates a series of varied microclimates. By allocating parks, gardens and other productive surfaces three-dimensionally, these microclimates create a new network of green spaces to provide the city with food, energy and social and cultural interactions.

L'ordre est dans l'individu, à la clef.
   multiplie ses effets quand l'individu se multiplie.

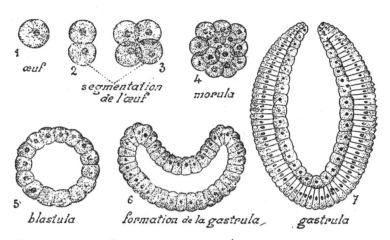

Fig. 49 à 55. — Développement d'une Éponge simple à partir de
l'œuf; les figures 1 à 3 sont à un plus fort grossissement que les
figures 4 à 7 (vu au microscope).

A HISTORY OF TERRITORIES, MOVEMENTS AND BORDERS
POLITICS OF INHABITATION

Un principe clair apporte la complexité simple (évolution).

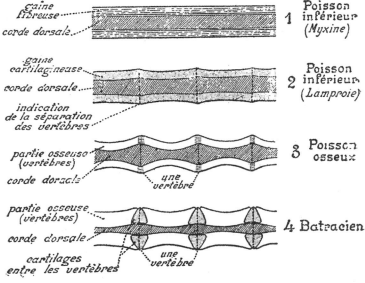

Fig. 167 à 170. — Colonnes vertébrales coupées en long, de plus en plus compliquées, chez les Poissons et les Batraciens.

If the city is as much about culture as nature, then a cultural understanding of the shaping of the urban is as essential as a scientific one. Here, architect and critic **Marina Lathouri,** who directs the graduate programme in History and Critical Thinking at the Architectural Association (AA) School of Architecture in London, describes how the concept of planning in the 19th century became intrinsically linked to notions of territory, borders and spatial organisation. She questions whether this might now be tested, and new design technologies used, to expose underlying emerging patterns of disruptive flows beckoning the possibility of the logic of a new social disposition.

When in 1926 the Swiss architect Hannes Meyer referred to the city as 'the most complex biological agglomeration' that 'must be consciously regulated and constructively shaped by man', and the dwelling unit (in this case the mass-produced house) as its 'living cell', the modern metropolis was already large and programmatically complex.[1] What architects and planners sought to develop at the time was a method to integrate the design of systems of inhabitation with processes of production of a larger territory; in short, principles and design techniques capable of operating across a number of scales. A number of specifically urban variables were recast as the fundamental problem of design, now supported by a new field of knowledge made up of disciplines ranging from statistics to sociology, economics to biology and design to engineering.

In this sense, many of the early propositions for the functional city, often discussed (and criticised) as statements of a utopian intent, were hardly iconic descriptions of an ideal city; rather they provided analytical constructs of the ways in which programmatic and architectural elements on the one hand, and economic and technical variants on the other, could be unified around an idea of dwelling in the city. Urban dwelling, which was the programmatic heading, was not so much concerned with either the domestic or the urban in terms of spatial scale as it was with the economy and culture of the urban in the future. It projected the ideals of a different relationship between the individual, the social and the city, between the singular and an ever-growing multitude.[2]

What comes to us today, at a time when the urban enclave and rise of global alternatives coexist, producing different forms of urban inhabitation and notions of community, is the demand to find new ways of approaching the same questions. In fact, a particular challenge in the work of identifying current dynamics and practices is that it is too often absorbed into conceptual frameworks that obscure their historical settings.

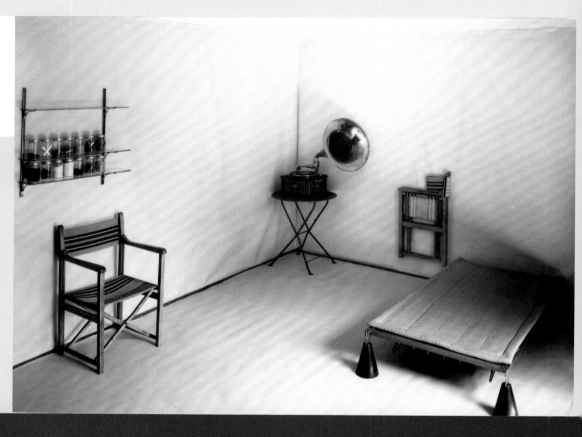

Hannes Meyer, Co-op Zimmer, 1926
The framed view of an interior, to be inhabited by what Meyer described as the 'semi-nomad of our modern productive system', is an arrangement (rather than a defined architectural space) of a set of standardised objects, signs of modernity which project a new way of living in the city, namely the idea of transient domesticity.

Systems

Reflection on the city was historically situated in a space of economic and administrative relations, and not solely on the basis of the symbolic relationship between a geometrical figure and the territory. Yet in the 19th century the city came to be thought of as an open and dynamic system, its planning essentially linked to patterns of distribution of land and population and forms of spatial organisation. This is in fact the meaning of the term 'planning' when it was first used by Ildefons Cerdà in his 1867 *Teoría General de la Urbanización* (*General Theory of Urbanization*) study, which he wrote to support his 1859 project for the extension of Barcelona.[3] According to Cerdà, 'planning' (and 'plan') indicated not a form but an activity, the process of forecasting and regulating change and growth, a type of urban development based on the management through design of the indeterminacy of economic, social, cultural and environmental forces.

The term 'planning' was also associated with the French '*distribuer*', meaning 'to apportion between several', and '*disposer*', 'to arrange, to put things in a certain order'.[4] These definitions may seem simple, but their implications are complex. Planning, as a practice and as a discipline of space, came to embrace everything from the tiniest physical entity to the whole territory; a range of scales that can be organised upon the same system of principles so that the effects of such ordering are potentially global. The primary rationale in these processes of expanding from the scale of the intimate to the geographical is 'capitalising a territory' over time rather than structuring space contained within a defined programmatic (functional) field.[5] In the case of Barcelona, the objective was to develop a plan with no definite limits that would apply to the entire region while outlining the future growth of the city.[6]

Central to this way of conceiving and programming the city is the idea of mobility – geographical, social and economic. It is not a coincidence that the problem of circulation and, in particular, the imagery of flow integrating a natural given with economy and efficiency has been most instrumental in modern and current design technologies. Cerdà, for example, positioned human nature between residence (*séjour*) and movement (*mouvement*), two categories essential to contemporaneous disciplines, namely biology and philosophy, and eventually the two cardinal functions around which all the constituent elements of urban reality ought to be organised. From then on, one could argue, this fundamental dichotomy of inhabitation/mobility becomes a new semiotics of human topology in the sense that it does not simply describe particular places and infrastructures, but signifies the relationship between people and territory connecting patterns of use with forms of spatial arrangement.

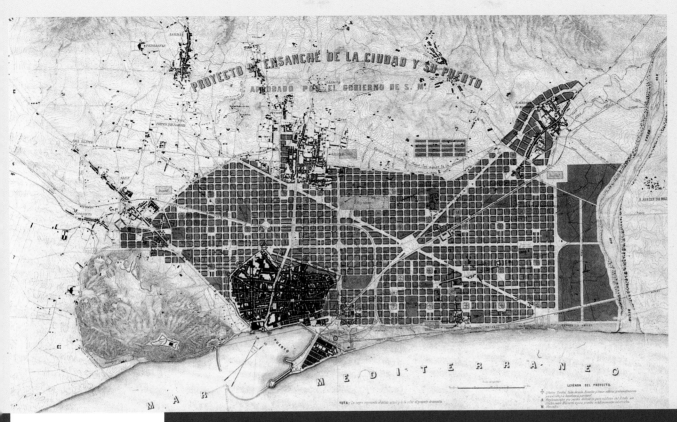

Ildefons Cerdà, Plan for the extension of the city of Barcelona, 1859
The plan, giving prominence to issues of spatial organisation of an expanding city, is no longer the representation of an ideal spatial, political or social order; it distributes, demarcates and organises individual elements formalising a type of urban development.

Borders

What if the history of modern planning was reorganised around the architectural question of connections and demarcations rather than uninterrupted flows and infrastructural systems? In fact, scholars have argued that making borders is an essentially modern gesture: ancient empires and medieval states had fluid and flexible borders, or none at all, and people lived and thrived in what were, in every sense, grey areas.[7] The growth of the nation state made the border an indispensable bureaucratic tool of mind and body control. Borders tell us where we stand, and where to stand.

In many ways, the primacy of border is about terrain and territory, the identification and definition of areas of interiority and proximity. This point is made clear when we understand the role of '*termini*', which could be translated as 'boundary stones', in the earliest narratives of the founding of Rome. These stones, which demarcated the '*limen*' (limits) within which all things were under the authority of Rome and subjected to Roman law, also

According to Cerdà, 'planning' (and 'plan') indicated not a form but an activity, the process of forecasting and regulating change and growth, a type of urban development based on the management through design of the indeterminacy of economic, social, cultural and environmental forces.

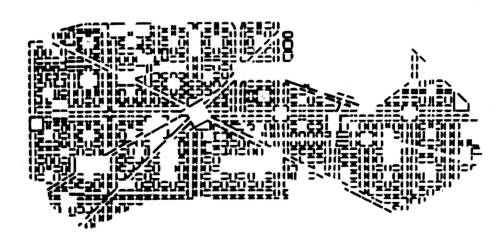

It is within the micro-geography of the diverse interfaces between the private and the public, and the individual and the collective, that the legal, spatial and biological intermingle.

marked the boundaries of individual properties. The passage from the private sphere of the household (*oikos*) and its economy (*oiko-nomia* – the law of the household) to the common (that is, the sovereign field), and the constitution through the practice of law of the body of citizens and therefore of the territory of the city, poses the question of border less as an act of delimitation than as a process of articulation of a multiplicity of economies.

It is within the micro-geography of the diverse interfaces between the private and the public, and the individual and the collective, that the legal, spatial and biological intermingle. This becomes important when one considers the principle of flow, which, while resting on the open and dynamic nature of contemporary processes of economic and cultural activity, also engenders novel forms of citizenship and transforms the city paradoxically into a permanent frontier zone. Though the structuring function of both mobility and connectivity involves fastening together and mutually reinforcing a multiplicity of territories and operations,

circulation systems and flows are inscribed within these territories and therefore involve geographical and social divisions. Inherent to the imagery of flow is not a smooth continuity as often argued. On the contrary, it consists in the ceaseless moving of the boundaries, a repudiation of geography and a very literal disruption of the relation between people and territory.

Whereas the broader principle of distribution and flow systems enable, at least in their field of application and in the techniques they call for, the larger, potentially global terrain of urbanisation, specific programmatic and cultural configurations articulate often-contested representations of that globality. The question that needs to be posed in the context of new forms of urban research should therefore concern the varying demarcations of these configurations, the ways in which their internal economies constitute interrelated yet distinct systems.

It is precisely there that new design technologies can play a role, in the articulation rather than the management of

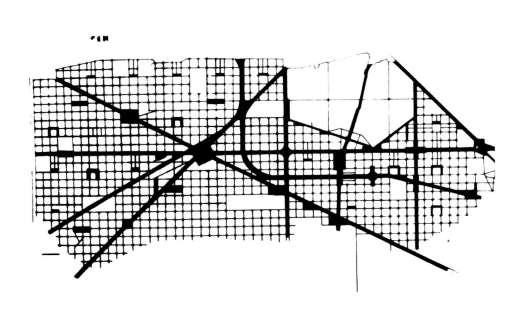

the indeterminacy. This does not contradict the dynamic potential of these technologies; rather, it calibrates the need to define (rather than deprive of any limit) and to circumscribe accordingly the intimate, the proximate, the common and the social. Would this mean that the emerging patterns would underlie the logic of a new social disposition, one going beyond the politics of culture and identity? Old ideologies have been thrown out, geopolitical structures have been displaced and globalisation is at work, but the architectural possibilities and political ramifications of this question ought to continue to be systematically investigated. ᴐ

Notes
1. Hannes Meyer, 'The New World' [1926], in Tim and Charlotte Benton with Dennis Sharp (eds), *Form and Function, A Source Book for the History of Architecture and Design 1890–1939: An International Anthology of Original Articles,* Crosby Lockwood Staples in association with the Open University Press (London), 1975, p 108.
2. As Le Corbusier put it, the dwelling unit is 'the architectural model of a *system* of inhabitation, of a cellular unit susceptible to vitality which can easily develop into the *urban fact'.* Le Corbusier, *Almanach d'architecture moderne,* Les Éditions G Crès & Cie (Paris), 1925, p 111.
3. Ildefons Cerdà, *Teoria General de la Urbanización y aplicación de sus principios y doctrinas a la reforma y ensanche de Barcelona* (Madrid), 1867. A more recent edition was published by Nabu Press in 2012. Ildefons Cerdà (1815–76), engineer, architect and the designer of the 1859 extension plan for Barcelona (known as the Eixample), also coined the term 'urbanism' and was the first theoretician of the discipline as science.

4. See Pierre Merlin and Françoise Choay, *Dictionnaire de l'urbanisme et de l'aménagement,* Presses Universitaires de France (Paris), 1988.
5. Michel Foucault, *Security, Territory, Population: Lectures at the Collège de France, 1977–1978,* Picador (New York), 2007, p 17. First edition: Éditions du Seuil/Gallimard (Paris), 2004.
6. See Cornelis van Eesteren, *The Idea of the Functional City,* NAi Publishers (Rotterdam), 1997. The text of the book is based on a lecture that van Eesteren delivered at the Dutch De Opbouw architectural association in Rotterdam in 1927. For van Eesteren, designer of the Amsterdam General Extension Plan (1934) and chairman of the Congrès internationaux d'architecture moderne (CIAM) from 1930 to 1947, planning was the necessary means to regulate and shape the continuing growth of human settlements.
7. See Alexander C Diener and Joshua Hagen, *Borders: A Very Short Introduction,* Oxford University Press (Oxford), 2012.

Liam Young and Kate Davies

A DISTRIB
GROUND

UTED

THE UNKNOWN FIELDS DIVISION

Chris Jordan, Circuit Boards, Atlanta, 2004
Image from photographer Chris Jordan's series 'Intolerable Beauty: Portraits of American Mass Consumption'.

As leaders of the Unknown Fields Division at the Architectural Association (AA) School of Architecture in London, **Liam Young and Kate Davies** take their students on trips to the end of the earth. Cataloguing extreme territories, they investigate the role of design in developing new cultural relationships. Fictional speculation is used as an instrument for understanding emerging environmental and technological futures, in a process of experiencing, chronicling and, ultimately, reimagining the urban and the remote, and charting global flows and trajectories. Here they describe a speculative supply chain that begins below the surface of the Western Desert in outback Australia, and continues to the Arctic 'Northwest Passage' and on to London.

Far from the metropolis lie the dislocated hinterlands that support the mechanisations of modern living. A city like London is thoroughly embedded in a global network of landscapes and infrastructures that are too often forgotten, unseen or ignored. The Unknown Fields Division is a nomadic design studio that ventures out on biannual expeditions to the ends of the earth to explore extreme landscapes, alien terrains and industrial ecologies. With groups of students and embedded collaborators, it re-imagines the complex realities of the present as a site of critical and speculative futures. It aims to remap the city and the technologies it contains not as discrete, independent collections of buildings and technologies, but as a networked object that conditions and is conditioned by a wide array of local and global landscapes. By developing an atlas of these supply chains, from consumption all the way back to their source in the ground, we can begin to understand the complex connections that exist between our everyday lives and a wider global context.

> Hunters for gold, pursuers of fame, they had all gone out on that stream … what greatness had not floated on the ebb of that river into the mystery of an unknown earth! … The dreams of men, the seed of commonwealths, the germs of empires.[1]

In *Heart of Darkness* (first published in 1899), Joseph Conrad sets the narrator of the story, Marlow, on a boat on the Thames, with the city glistening serenely behind him, recalling a voyage into the unknown. In doing so he sets the familiar world of the city in direct relation to the distant continent in which his voyage into darkness unravels. The exact location of this voyage remains obscure in Conrad's text, uncertain next to the certainty of the departure point. The 'biggest and the greatest town on earth',[2] the site from which he embarks – the known from which we relate to the unknown – might be read as the true ground for the narrative. It is both departure point and backdrop; 'and this also,' says Marlow suddenly, 'has been one of the dark places of the earth.'[3] 'Here' and 'there' are woven together, and when the familiar is implicated in the framing of the unfamiliar, 'where do we come from?' is as important as 'where are we going?'. It is this dialogue between the immediate and the remote that is always at the centre of the work of the Unknown Fields Division.

The emphasis of Unknown Fields' research is to catalogue these sites as a productive process. In order to speculate on how design may play a role in developing new cultural relationships with the inevitable by-products of industry, a changing climate and the 'anthropocenic' world, we first need to attempt to understand that world by bearing witness to some of these emerging infrastructural landscapes. These territories must be lived, experienced and chronicled, but ultimately they must also be re-imagined. This complex web of interconnections and landscapes that gives shape to our world is too intricate to fully understand, but through storytelling and designed scenarios we can start to relate to that complexity in meaningful ways, and we can use these imaginative leaps to test our responses to possible futures.

For Unknown Fields, the journey is the site along which we construct a series of parallel narratives and partial fabrications, chronicling some probable fictions we have imagined in response to the improbable truths we have witnessed. As architects we have the ability to construct realities for others to inhabit, to help shape cultural narratives and inform the way we collectively think about the world. When considering these landscapes it is critical that we engage with the stories we construct as a culture around them. Whether through political spin, science fiction, nature documentary, environmental protest, disaster film, fairytale, folklore or scientific analysis, these narratives are many and varied. By understanding the mythology and stories of these distant landscapes and disrupting or intervening within them as a 'second site', we can bridge a gap between the here and there.

Traversing a Speculative Supply Chain

We narrate here a scenic journey with the Unknown Fields Division along a speculative supply chain. It is a field guide through the science-fictional landscapes of the present, the landscapes of technology and the technologies of landscape. It is a trajectory woven from some of the very real physical sites the Division has explored across the last few years. Stitching these places together forms a new territory for us to inhabit, a city of logistics and trajectories, of shifting resources and distributed ground. It is a space that is at once nowhere and everywhere.

The Unknown Fields supply chain begins 1 kilometre (0.6 miles) below the surface crust of the earth. The ground steams and rumbles as the division stands in a new shaft of the Wiluna Gold Mine, on the edge of the Western Desert in outback Australia. Unknown Fields will follow the material of this excavated landscape of caves and canyons as it is scattered

Christina Seely, Arctic ice shelf, Barrow, Alaska, 2011
Unknown Fields stands on the frozen Arctic Ocean as their expedition plane makes its landing run in the sky above.

Wiluna Gold Mine, Wiluna, Western Australia, 2010
On its Western Australia expedition, the Unknown Fields Division stands 1 kilometre (0.6 miles) below the ground at Wiluna Gold Mine, a huge hole in the ground that is a material consequence of a culturally constructed fiction: the gold price.

Super Pit, Kalgoorlie, Western Australia, 2010
During the Unknown Fields 'Never Never Lands' expedition, the Division stands on the edge of the Kalgoorlie Super Pit gold mine.

Super Pit night mining, Kalgoorlie, Western Australia, 2010
Unknown Fields watches the mining operations continue uninterrupted throughout the night in an effort to maximise production.

across the earth. We each have a little piece of Wiluna on us now, in our pockets; 0.034 grams (0.001 pounds) of it is locked away in our mobile phones. We travel up through the gold fields and monster iron-ore mines, following the 2-kilometre (1.2-mile) trains that drag the mountains out of the Australian outback and onto colossal ships bound for China to build cities for a rapidly urbanising population. Here lies the shadow of those cities, the silent twin: the void where a landform once was. These are the dislocated resource sites that support the world that we are more familiar with. Australia is a landscape whose material has been exploded into a global constellation, from iron ore for the pop-up cities in China, to bauxite for aluminium smelting in Iceland, uranium powering UK nuclear reactors, gold-plated connections in supercomputers modelling climate change in Alaska, food-grade titanium paint marking 'm&m' on confectionary in a convenience store in Los Angeles, and diamonds for sharpening knives in a sushi restaurant in Tokyo.

This vast infrastructural geology is cut out of the narrative landscape that embodies the creation stories of the Aboriginal Australians. Aboriginal dreamtime narratives speak of a time when the ground was soft and creation beings shaped mountains and rivers. When the rainbow serpent slinked across the ground to create a river, and a wild dog came to rest to form a mountain. Stories and ceremonies of dreaming beings that once shaped the sacred sites of ranges and riverbeds are now spun with the ghosts of modern technologies. Explosives, diggers and drills have replaced the slow erosion of rivers and winds. The division follows a railway to Port Headland where iron ore is stockpiled for export to China. Here we meet the Aboriginal painter Lorraine Sampson, standing in the red dust blown from the carriages, 'watching the trains take her country away'.

Mining survey planes track back and forth, laser scanning the earth searching for the topographic anomalies that indicate pockets of undiscovered minerals on the ground. The scans locate a field to be core sampled, creating a geological map of the ore body below ground, a void in waiting. Traditional paintings of dreamtime stories have often been used to support land rights claims, set in relation to the narrative of a fluctuating market that also lays claim to this landscape. The technologies with which this ground is surveyed and recorded also become the political means through which groups claim ownership over it.

As the Unknown Fields Division heads further along the supply chain we visit the Wiluna mine design office in Perth and watch the shape of the excavation change as the variable gold price is entered into the engineering software. As the gold price rises, it becomes more economical to mine areas of lower gold-ore concentration. As the price drops, the virtual mine shrinks as the software focuses the next cut around deposits of richer gold ore. Cut by cut, the fluctuations of the gold price are etched into the ground of Western Australia at the scale of the Grand Canyon. This steamy black void in which the division previously stood is a live graph, a wormhole

shaped by the frequency of electronic trades in London and New York. The gold is extracted from this ancient ground so it can be quantified and weighed. It is then shipped across the world from one hole in the ground to another as it is stored below the surface once more in the vaults of HSBC or the Federal Reserve. Here the majority of this material remains, to be traded virtually. The gold's value is a fiction, embodied by a block of material wrung like blood from a stone from vast tracts of earth to end, sitting trapped, back in the earth.

This is a landscape of conflicting narratives and value systems that raise difficult questions about our role as custodians. We continue along the mineral train line, rumbling towards the vast ports of the Western Australian coast. Everything in Port Headland is painted red. Everything is dusted in the rich ochre of the interior, blown from the top of stockpiles and the loaders that are filling immense ships bound for distant lands. Tanker by tanker an ancient landscape is being atomised and redistributed.

From here, bauxite mined in the Western Australian outback is shipped as alumina to the edge of the Arctic to harvest Iceland's outpouring of energy for aluminium smelting. We travel with it to this next stop on the supply chain, a landscape mined for its energy. In Iceland, an excess of geothermal energy means that this island is an oasis in a region shaped by power consumption. They are harvesting energy at 3 cents per kilowatt-hour in relation to the rest of the world where production ranges from 7 to 20 cents per kilowatt-hour, and Iceland is rushing to create new industries to put it to use. This 'clean' energy means it is economically viable to ship raw material, extracted half a world away, here for processing only to send it back across the planet again. Alcoa runs a plant near the town of Reydarfjördur, which contains a hydropower station with twice the energy output as all those used to power the rest of the country put together. Iceland's unique resources mean the conversation about energy is at odds with the usual narratives.

Iceland is 30 milliseconds from Alaska – via the FARICE-1 and Arctic Fibre undersea data cables. The Unknown Fields Division clicks 'cheap flights Alaska', two price-comparison windows open and we contemplate our carbon footprint, but not for the reasons you might think. The servers that enact this search consume approximately the same amount of energy it takes to boil water for a cup of coffee. The carbon footprint of the IT industry is set to overtake the airline industry by 2020, and Internet giants and their server farm empires are the other new industries starting to capitalise on Iceland's 'guilt-free' energy. These machines need little beside cool temperatures and cheap power. Here the cloud of digital technology is caught feeding, and the arctic north is becoming the home of the world's data. The ephemera of the cloud, the invisible web of connections finds an extraordinary physical form in the volcanic deserts of Iceland. Standing beside the vast server racks, our faces are illuminated by thousands of blinking LEDs, flashing with

Iron ore shipping, Port Headland, Western Australia, 2010
Unknown Fields films from their expedition sailboat as tankers are loaded with iron ore to be shipped to the instant cities of China.

Hellisheidi Geothermal Power Plant, Hengill, Iceland, 2009
Unknown Fields is lost in geothermal steam as the station harnesses the energy that now fuels Iceland's growing aluminium-smelting and data-server industries.

Jökulsárlón glacier lagoon, Iceland, 2009
Unknown Fields clamber across broken fragments of the Vatnajökull glacier as they drift back and forth, trapped in a lake of melt water.

Pacman Supercomputer, University of Fairbanks, Alaska, 2011
At the University of Fairbanks, the group listens to the Pacman supercomputer calculate the possible climate futures of the Arctic Refuge.

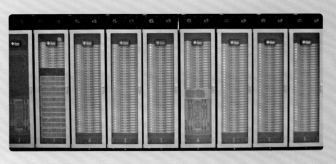

every email, search, naughty chat and magnum opus. This ethereal landscape laced with folklore and boiling beneath with energy in abundance is the incubator for new stories we may tell ourselves.

The Arctic region is more familiar as the protagonist in current environmental narratives and a territory in which we find the complexities and contradictions of the energy debate playing out. Unknown Fields follows the data stream, an information supply chain, from one Arctic information hub to another, from geothermal warehouses to a large white room in Fairbanks, Alaska. At the Arctic Region Supercomputing Center we meet a supercomputer called 'Pacman' with its banks of parallel processors, performing trillions of operations per second, flanked by entire rooms full of data tapes, each one full of readings and measurements, extrapolated figures and complex computational models. Mindboggling numbers are involved as these computational behemoths carry out their task of predicting the future. This is a major hub in a global feedback system, assessing and predicting the effect of human activity on the planet's ecology. Reminding us that now as never before our actions in a city like London have huge implications on a faraway landscape we may never visit. Pacman computes climate and weather forecasts, modelling sea-ice formation, Arctic Ocean dynamics, ecological systems and resource depletion. It is from places like these that we are relayed news of pressing environmental concerns as the complexity of the natural world and our thirst for certainty about long- and short-term futures requires ever-finer resolution and ever-greater computing power.

In a cafe in Anchorage we meet an oil lobbyist for Arctic Power. He discusses the future of the Arctic National Wildlife Refuge (ANWR), arguing that the US has no option but to drill there. To support his claim, he reels off an exhausting list of products made from oil: the plastic spoon in his hand, the fertiliser for the food we are eating, our medicines, cosmetics and clothes among others. The computed figures and predictions convince him that the ANWR will one day produce a million barrels a day. Others interpret the same figures very differently. What is revealed to us is a stretch of landscape in Northern Alaska caught in a state of becoming. That is, becoming part of a supply chain. It is an irreplaceable haven for wildlife earmarked as a future oil field. It is monitored by environmentalists and speculators alike and is a space woven with conflicting forecasts for its future.

Our supply chain comes to an end in a landscape in limbo at the top of the world. We land on the icy runway at Barrow, on the far north coast of Alaska, at winter solstice, and we slip into the darkness of an endless night. We stand on the frozen Arctic Ocean, its landward edge illuminated by street lights along the shorefront. This is the landscape Pacman is thinking about. Here, climate scientists and Inuit work together to divine the future of this landscape. They watch this place. The Inuit compile ice diaries from careful observation and share ancestral knowledge, and scientists consult delicate instrumentation and differ in their outlook fundamentally.

There is a thick streak of determined pragmatism from the Inuit community whose attitude as a culture is to approach change with confidence in their own ability to adapt and so embrace multiple future scenarios with openness and resourcefulness. At the same time environmental scientists assemble their observations into climate forecasts with the hope of predicting the future as precisely as possible. The Far North is a landscape as a science experiment, a predictive model of itself that informs the future strategies of global environmental and energy policies that are penned back in the metropolises it supports. A distant landscape conditioned by, and conditioning, the cities closer to home. A landscape mined for data as well as resources. A landscape measured in retreating ice and remaining barrels of oil. It is a supply-chain territory, precious and fragile, violent and terrifying.

Returning Home
As we come to the end of our travelogue, from the 'Antipodes' to the 'Northwest Passage', we are reminded again that our point of view – the here from which we relate to there – is a large part of the story. It is interesting to note that both of these terms presume an origin in Northern Europe: 'Antipodal' being the point diametrically opposite a given location on the globe, and 'Northwest' assuming a Southeast from which to view it. We are aware that connections may tell a more accurate story than the nodes.

This has been a narrative voyage through just a few of the sites we have visited with the Unknown Fields Division over the last four years. Sites that offer us a new perspective from which to understand the emerging conditions we are designing for. Landscapes where we find the future in the present tense, and which act as condensers of wider issues that we relate to only in an abstract sense in our more familiar cities. They are places on the margins of our knowledge where issues such as climate change, depleting resources, declining biodiversity, pervasive technologies and so on play out with more immediacy and more urgency. They provide us glimpses into alternative futures and form test beds for designers to critically evaluate the implications of emerging technologies.

Architects operate in the fertile ground between culture, nature and technology. We are in a unique position to synthesise diverse and complex factors, to pose alternative scenarios and counter-narratives, and communicate them with imagination and precision. An aim of Unknown Fields is to prototype different ways of thinking about and acknowledging this complexity. If we can reveal this hidden cartography, we can begin to acknowledge the interconnected nature of 'place' and explore new ways to start to navigate through a complicated planet. We are a generation privileged enough to be able to bear witness to this emerging world, and this is a powerful place to be – on the very edge of the potential for change. ∆

Satellite dish array, Barrow, Alaska, 2011
An array of communications dishes on the edge of town beams data back to the cities in the South.

Living on the edge of the world, Barrow, Alaska, 2011
For the winter solstice, Unknown Fields stays in the scientist quarters on the coast of the Arctic Ocean.

Research station, Barrow, Alaska, 2011
The Unknown Fields Division approaches a distant scientific research station on the coast of the Arctic Ocean.

Notes
1. Joseph Conrad, *Heart of Darkness*. Penguin Classics (London), 2007, p 5.
2. Ibid.
3. Ibid

THIRD NATURES

Cristina Díaz Moreno and Efrén García Grinda

INCUBATORS OF PUBLIC SPACE

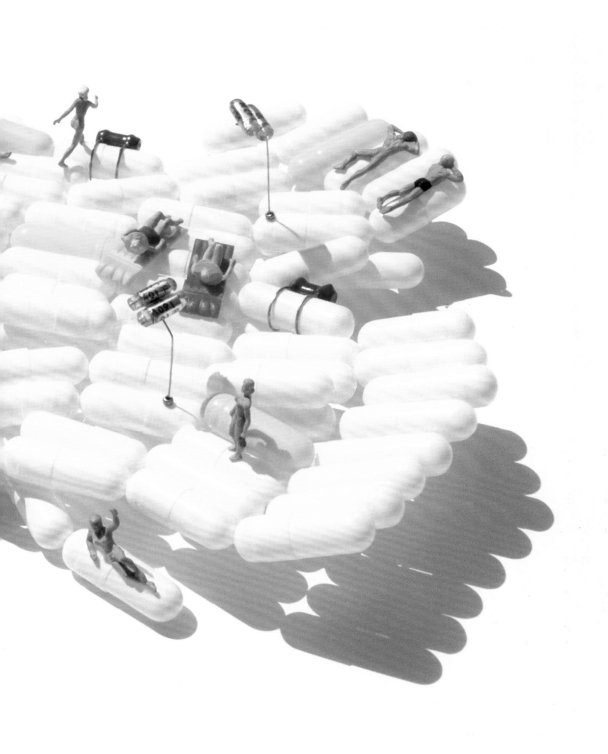

AMID.cero9, 4S: Sun Sand, Sea, Sex, Bruges, Belgium, 2002
Reactivating the romantic, medieval European tourist destination of Bruges, the project
here extends the city's network of canals, introducing a series of floating artificial oases
conceived as generators of pleasures. These large heated platforms create hedonistic
micro-enclaves that serve as artificially generated replicas of Mediterranean beaches.

Cristina Díaz Moreno and Efrén García Grinda, founders of the Madrid-based office AMID.cero9, shift the notion of the urban from the classic idea of the complete or ideal city, to one which engages with essential urban phenomena: the dynamics of confrontation, dispute and agreement between individuals, social groups and subcultures. In this way, public spaces are transformed from empty spaces into a real context for social interaction; and active involvement with social exchange becomes the main purpose of a project for a new architecture of the city.

Never before has the city been the focus of so much attention, not only from anthropologists, architects and sociologists, but also as an important fixture in the agendas of politicians and economists. Modern urban development processes are usually defined as the main result of the late capitalist society, of its cycles and its logic, and they are identified with it. However, arguments about urban elements today portray these elements as a general, universal and all-enveloping condition that we inhabit, and in which it is not possible to intervene as architects, rather than as an object of a project or for discussion. Every approach to urban phenomena seems to be guided by the analysis, criticism and fascination that they produce instead of by the creation of alternative models. Are cities thus a mere scenario for our activities, or can we view them as part of our scope of action?

Let us cast our minds back almost 2,400 years: Aristotle's view of the city was established in the first two chapters of *Politics* as the meeting point for the various *oikos*, for people from different places and families. The process of creation of the first cities is defined as '*synoikismos*', literally, the process whereby different *oikos* would form a city by deciding to live together to provide mutual protection and assistance: a continuous process of living together and discussing mutual hopes and benefits. Cities then became a gathering of people that were not the same or similar, but different individuals in reciprocal equality. They accepted they had to coexist under the same system of rules in a tacit and ongoing process of negotiation and interaction, agreements and disagreements, more than a physically complete thing.

Francesco Colonna, *Hypnerotomachia Poliphili*, 1499
This illustrated incunabulum translated into English as *Poliphilo's Strife of Love in a Dream* introduced an erotic fantasy in the form of a journey that is driven forward by the constant deciphering of temples, gardens, fountains, ruins, inscriptions or frescoes.

André Adolphe Eugène Disdéri, *Communards in their Coffins*, Paris, 1871
The Paris Commune acted as the local authority in Paris for two months in the spring of 1871, a result of an uprising in the city after the French were defeated in the Franco-Prussian war. The uprising was the model for most of the revolutionary utopias of the 20th century, and was violently suffocated in the *Semaine Sanglante* (Bloody Week) ending on the 28 May.

However, beyond the concept of the origin of the city and its pertinence today, modern urban environments are nowhere near being peaceful and harmonious melting pots of diversity, where social identity is supposedly built upon equal participation between different elements. Urban agglomerations are not only home for differences, but also host and provoke violence, conflicts and inequality. Consensus and equitable participation are only two of the possible scenarios that can arise from the dispute between different ways of life. Control, marginalisation and violence are others, as is the creation of elective communities, such as social groups or subcultures, which argue against mainstream cultural structures through style and the public exposure of alternative ways of life. Both direct forms of negotiation and interaction (for example, urban revolts of discontent) and mediated or indirect forms (public exposure of alternative aesthetics) are extreme examples of the range of potential manifestations of the constant public redefinition of social constructs.

Thus, urban environments can be considered a fascinating phenomenon of ongoing dispute between different groups, a hub of conflictive economic and cultural exchanges in a highly artificialised and constructed environment. The possibility of again tackling the project of the city could hinge around displacing the purpose of the project. It would shift from the complete city, which is impossible to anticipate due to its complexity and temporary and accumulative nature, to an intervention at the core of the urban phenomenon: the dynamics of confrontation, dispute and agreement between individuals, social groups and subcultures, defining the physical location where they take place and taking this scenario of relationships as a real context. The real and physical public space would become the main purpose of a project for a new architecture of the city, the aim of which is to become actively involved in contemporary urban phenomena.

Thus, urban environments can be considered a fascinating phenomenon of ongoing dispute between different groups, a hub of conflictive economic and cultural exchanges in a highly artificialised and constructed environment.

Marisa González, *Filipinas en Hong Kong*, 2010
Marisa González's work attempts to track back the public activities of the 150,000 Filipino women who work as housekeepers in Hong Kong. Once a week, they invade the downtown financial district, transforming the streets, bridges, parks and plazas into a truly public domain on their only day off with their own habits, culture and traditions.

These processes are spatial phenomena by nature: they occur within, and generate, space. Therefore the true notion of the city can only emerge within and from a new notion of the term 'space'. Space can be defined as something that occurs between entities of different origins that coexist physically in a given place. It is not a thing, not a physical reality that happens out there, but instead a set of relationships under constant definition. It thus takes place among things, among an array of different elements that are being constantly transformed and reciprocating each other. It is a typical phenomenon of physical interaction and intermediation that defies the categories between subject and object. Everything is subject and object of the (inter)action at the same time, and everything participates in their definition. The concept of space that is usually associated with modernity, that white and empty canvas where all traces of biotic activity are cancelled in a physical and conceptual process of hygienisation, is displaced by a new notion that fosters the meeting, collision and richness of cultural materials. It is a new dirty, smelly and noisy place where different agents from different origins physically clash to undertake the constant rebuilding of the ethos of a given community through their actions.

Public space would then cease to be mechanically associated with emptiness – as opposed to the built-up urban factory – or with a space for free and universal access, and would become the space for the collision between dominating cultures and the new practices that try to discuss them. Being physically together and sharing space while at the same time collectively building the scene through public interaction becomes a process of constant identity review and reformulation for a given society, and therefore for the city itself. The pieces that compound the city would work as incubators of alternative ways of approaching the world that promote public dissidence, differences and the plurality of the origins of the intervening actors, embracing and inducing alternative ways of life that would be distant from the passive models of experience consumption. As an intermediation phenomenon, public space would then become defined not only by the architecture that contains it, but also by the actions of users and of the people that inhabit it: a meeting place for people of all classes and

origins – humans, non-humans, inert objects, biotic materials, physical and virtual technologies – in constant interaction. These are what we call 'third natures'.[1]

This type of space exists in reality, but it appears surreptitiously and spontaneously in the city, in places of exchange and interaction. Despite their elusive nature, there are some situations – assemblies of people, actions and physical buildings – where the ideal of the political notion of public space materialises in physical and real spaces. The safe spaces of lesbian, gay, transgender and bisexual (LGTB) communities, squatted buildings, camps, positive ghettos of elective communities, riots, demonstrations, festivals or the hostile occupation of public spaces involve the appropriation of territories whose use and identity is highly undetermined. This open and uncertain nature leads to active occupation, transformation and spatial adaptation practices, and

AMID.cero9 with José Quintanar and Colectivo Cuartoymitad, The Big Mech and Co: Gran Vía Toxic, Madrid, 2008–10
top: Gran Vía Toxic provides a scenario within which to discuss the methods of cultural and material production of the city, and the economical and political implications of the contemporary process of urbanisation, through destruction processes.

bottom: In recent years the housing and property market has generated a disproportionate and unjustified increase in poor-quality buildings, resulting in an exponential growth in the historic substandard materiality of the city. The proposal here therefore looks for opportunities in the destruction of the urban fabric and the treatment of its waste, to create a reverse process of urban transformation that might ultimately transform the city.

Space can be defined as something that occurs between entities of different origins that coexist physically in a given place.

usually goes hand in hand with the physical decay and ruin that elective communities or subcultures feed upon to negotiate their identity, as they constantly experiment with new lifestyles.[2] They are unaware of the deterministic forces of capital, property, standardisation and institutionalisation, and build new spatial enclaves, real outsides within the physical inside of the city, where new notions of the public scope are collectively developed.

Since there is a general lack of available space within the city, these manifestations can migrate to waste landscapes, deserts or, in the words of Bruce Sterling, 'involuntary parks'.[3] The functional decadence and obsolescence of these spaces make them alternatives for non-conventional forms of collectivity, and their conflictive and non-conventional use of cultural forms (for example, parties, flash mobs, carnivals or artistic performances, all of which oppose production and routine, that is, the counter-routine) to stage the dissensus are indirect and sophisticated forms of dissidence that replace direct political discussion and negotiation. These new ways of group participation explore and celebrate cultural particularities, they aim to make physical and aesthetic marks, and also to deal with the profound contemporary aestheticisation of experience and ways of life.

A question inevitably follows: how can architecture as a discipline contribute to the creation of physical public spaces of a political nature, and hence to the project of a city as a public space for the interrelation between various social actors, and as the physical reality that houses and induces them?

Back in the present, it is necessary to think about what new displacement of our culture of the project is needed to again tackle the issue of urban phenomena through these third natures. The way elective communities, subcultures or social groups emphatically and critically discuss the dominating culture provides some suggestions. Assembly, network, revolt, camp and festival are the new models and figures of this kind of space: a synchronised collectivity of interacting individuals within the constraints, limits and physical barriers of the city, in a horizontal and potentially equitable communicative interaction between individuals. This interaction takes the form of a transformation or physical, and sometimes

AMID.cero9 with José Quintanar and Colectivo Cuartoynitad, The Big Mech and Co: Gran Via Toxic, Madrid, 2008–10
top: This social engineering of a clinical order can be read as a brutal example of the 'creative destruction' concept developed by the Economist Joseph Alois Schumpeter in his book *Capitalism, Socialism and Democracy* (1942). According to his thesis, modernity is an eminently creative destructive process supported by a constant succession of innovations. Drawing by Ja Ja Ja.

AMID.cero9, The Magic Mountain, Ames, Iowa, 2002
bottom: A former power station is wrapped in an ecosystem mask that converts energy infrastructures and architecture into a living system to be inserted within the city. The membrane attracts the most important butterfly and bird species in the northern US like a real mountain, and the building is converted into the laboratory of a genetic engineer, where different species and varieties of roses can be researched and developed, challenging the common tools and concepts of architecture, gardening, species breeding and the ecology of living.

violent, occupation of the city. It ultimately combines pleasure, creativity and political resistance in a temporary explosion of collective cultural and social impatience.[4]

Projecting a city through the definition of its public spaces also involves tackling and overcoming the schism and dilemma between belonging to the urban logic or assertion as an individual element. This conflict is the main source of frustration when faced with the challenge of the project of the city, but it could be neutralised by considering that the specific conditions of the independent elements that make it up can be defined with an implicit city logic, thus discussing the role of buildings as discrete and finite elements. If cities can be considered a synchronised collectivity of independent elements, architecture should yield in some of its performative properties due to its belonging to an urban whole. In any case, not all the spatial formal and organisational characteristics need to be relinquished to the city, recovering the typological discourse and limiting the task of design to an abstract adaptation, to the specific contingencies of a context. Instead, the hyper-specificity of the elements needs to be exacerbated. All formal, geometrical, spatial and organisational decisions need to be linked to their cultural milieu, as established by the appearance of alternative cultural models, and they should only partially be subjected to the common urban condition. The level of permeability, accessibility, indetermination, connection with the city or the languages used is a matter of concern for this new architecture of the city. The capability of establishing culturally backed bonds with the cultural context through each decision would again grant architecture the ability to materialise as a highly specific object that reaffirms its identity as a unique and once-in-a-lifetime experiment. The project of the city can then find its place within the natural habitat of architecture and can be conceived as the definition of independent and finite pieces from an ocean of entities that act like a synchronised multitude.

The first of the complex interdependences between city and architecture where work can be done involves the continuity, connection and physical segregation of the built object with respect to its urban surroundings. Analysing ghettos as positive spatial models helps us

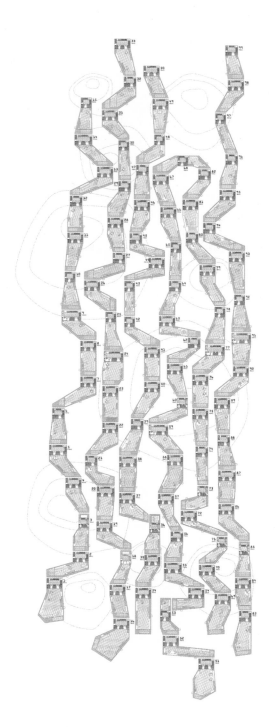

AMID.cero9, Southern Exposure, Jyväskylä, Finland, 2001
This organisation system of north–south strips of single housing units all facing onto a private courtyard and looking south produces spatial compressions and expansions that subdivide the continuous public space into small areas in such a way that the whole is characterised as a piece of the city and understood as a synchronised multitude of independent buildings.

understand how the project of the limit and the degree of exclusion of architecture can foster the appearance of new and alternative cultural lifestyles, and hence the extension of the public domain. 'Auto-inclusivity', that is, the selective physical isolation of a community, encourages the construction of the distinguishing features of that community's identity. It makes them aware of their own characteristics while at the same time constructing a safe haven for the collective reaffirmation of the group. This includes a discussion about their level of autonomy and the edge effect of the separating 'ecotone', that is, the physical barrier, the transition area between the inside and the city, the conflict area for two or more communities. These 'other' spaces are the breeding ground for new dissident cultural forms and alternative lifestyles. Understanding architecture as a spatial enclave, as an autonomous area with distinguishing features, which precisely defines its degree of inclusivity and continuity with the urban factory, is not in conflict with the public sphere. Instead, paradoxically, it reinforces it.

The first of the complex interdependences between city and architecture where work can be done involves the continuity, connection and physical segregation of the built object with respect to its urban surroundings.

AMID.cero9, The Gay Vatican, Mojave Desert, California, 2010
The Gay Vatican is an autonomous enclave with a distinct identity in the Mojave Desert for the lesbian, gay, transgender and bisexual (LGTB) community. It is a public space experiment that examines the development over time of the construction of the community and their seasonal behaviour. Drawing by Ja Ja Ja.

On the other hand, work on the level of interiorisation helps in the definition of the physical conditions of space and the programmes it houses, understood as the physical and temporary organisation of activities that can generate the necessary publicness. More than a behaviourist approach, the goal is to work on the space where various agents interact, firstly to summon the different actors and secondly to foster and house the active construction of public spaces. It would therefore be possible to present alternatives to the dominating forms of urbanisation and production of space, developing assemblies that critically argue about their level of exclusion and their distinctive spatial characteristics, which are based on the distinct cultures of the elective communities that inhabit the city and defined through the connections established with different cultural capitals and materials.

Bearing this in mind, it makes sense to abandon the languages normally associated with the architecture of the city.[5] Simplification, the anonymity of the elements or the zero degree of languages, were related to the subordination of the general standard because of their urban status, as a direct answer to the constant demand for differences and novelty. However, the wealth and variety of cultural and subcultural forms in our city environment allow us to contemplate the possibility of reintroducing language as a necessary link with cultural specificity. The result would be a type of 'afterpop' language,[6] where no distinction would be made between high-brow and popular culture, where the source for cultural materials would be consciously modulated to establish a biunivocal relationship between language, social groups, their rituals and activities and the built-up space. Instead of proposing a generic, anonymous and standard mass of urbanisation where language singularities or particular cultural connections are

AMID.cero9, Cherry Blossom Pavilion, Jerte Valley, Extremadura, Spain, 2008–
For the area's annual spring Cherry Blossom Festival, AMID.cero9 proposed the construction of a contemporary chapel that establishes a close bond with the surrounding landscape through its presence, position, volume and materials. The chapel will act as a future assembly of both natural and artificial elements: cherry trees, wildlife, tourists and inhabitants.

not required, the focus would shift to highly specific prototypes that are defined through their connections to a vast array of cultural materials.

The indirect understanding of the city project would therefore require each of the elements that make it up to be viewed as a prototype adapted to a specific scenario that defines a renewed model of the relationship with the city, and therefore that could potentially contain seeds for new and alternative models for the current process of global urbanisation. Working with urban elements does not mean submitting yet another new universal city model, with ideal projections of the future or negative visions presenting the consequences of the global urbanisation process. Instead, it means re-examining the capability of purely architectural decisions for each of the elements to indirectly put forward alternatives to institutionalised, regulated and standard urbanisation processes. These would thus be transformed into real spaces for discussion and become the breeding ground for alternative ways of life. In short, this new architecture of the city would be a constructed version of the interaction and dynamics of subcultural forms. ∆

Notes

1. The philosophy of the 'terza natura' (third nature) was introduced by Jacopo Bonfadio in the early 16th century to define the characteristics of the new kinds of garden spaces that were both natural and man-made, and in which historical references and mythology were essential features. These new entities were portrayed in Hypnerotomachia Poliphili, attributed to Leon Battista Alberti and written under the pen name of Francesco Colonna in 1499. See John Dixon Hunt, Greater Perfections: The Practice of Garden Theory, University of Pennsylvania Press (Philadelphia, PA), 2000.
2. Dougal Sheridan, 'The Space of Subculture in the City: Getting Specific about Berlin's Indeterminate Territories', Field, Vol 1, No 1, September 2007.
3. Bruce Sterling,'The World is Becoming Uninsurable, Part 3', Viridian Note 00023: see www.viridiandesign.org/notes/1-25/Note%20 00023.txt.
4. Manuel Delgado, El espacio Público como Ideología, Los libros de la Catarata (Madrid), 2011.
5. Pier Vittorio Aureli, The Possibility of an Absolute Architecture, MIT Press (Cambridge, MA), 2011.
6. Eloy Fernández Porta, Afterpop, La literatura de la implosión mediática, Editorial Berenice (Córdoba), 2007, and Homo Sampler, Tiempo y consumo en la Era Afterpop, Editorial Anagrama (Barcelona), 2008.

Instead of proposing a generic, anonymous and standard mass of urbanisation where language singularities or particular cultural connections are not required, the focus would shift to highly specific prototypes that are defined through their connections to a vast array of cultural materials.

As a building that can remain closed for months and open just for a few days for the spring festival or autumn season, in the same way as does a church on pilgrimage days, the Cherry Blossom Pavilion is a strange typology – a rare new species.

INTELLIGENT CITIES AND THE TAXONOMY OF COGNITIVE SCALES

Here, Guest-Editor **Michael Weinstock with Mehran Gharleghi** of the EmTech programme at the Architectural Association (AA) School of Architecture in London shift the definition of the intelligent city away from one that is predicated on information and communication technologies towards a deeper and more profound characterisation. They explore the possibilities of cognitive complexity in urbanism emerging out of the interaction of sensory processing and behavioural responses to the world. Within the context of large infrastructural systems, what might, for instance, rapidly developing machine consciousness have in common with collective intelligence? What could the preliminary conceptual schema be for an intelligent city that is sufficiently self-aware to synchronise its systems with climatic and ecological phenomena at regional and local scales?

There are many competing definitions of intelligent cities, but all tend to converge on information and communication technologies coupled to local computation embedded in the physical artefacts of urban infrastructures. Microprocessors, originally developed as components of computers, cameras, cars and phones are now beginning to be deployed in urban environments, and in combination with advances in sensors and data transmission are driving the evolution of urban information systems. From this perspective, intelligent cities are typically described as the collection of intelligent buildings, shared car and cycle mobility schemes, and various interactive information systems for municipal and privately supplied services and governance, and often linked to the development systems for the 'innovation economy'.

Cities such as Chicago and Amsterdam have current programmes underway to integrate and modify energy and water flows by the use of intelligent metering and building systems, and Sydney is implementing a network of distributed generators in a 'smart grid' that will, when completed in 2030, produce most of the city's power. Although the list of components may differ among the competing definitions of the intelligent city, none significantly addresses the concept and components of artificial intelligence, the specifics of the intelligence required for a city, nor the relations between separate sentient urban infrastructural systems and how they might be integrated into an intelligent metasystem.[1]

Although sensors are now ubiquitous in urban environments, there is as yet relatively little research within the sciences of the city[2] on the development of systems that integrate the data from sensors into a sentient system, and even less on how separate sentient systems can be integrated with each other and contribute to the cognitive complexity of intelligence. Even within the science of artificial intelligence, sentience remains a minor area of research. By contrast, in the biological sciences it is considered to be a primary attribute of intelligence, and it is widely understood that intelligence cannot emerge without it. Sentience is generally accepted to be the appropriate term for the ability to sense the world external to the organism; no organism can respond to its environment or become better adapted to it over time without sentience. Cognitive complexity emerges from the interaction of sensory processing and behavioural response to the world. Intelligence may be considered as the collection of behaviours that enable an organism to survive and thrive in its environment, and it therefore follows that sentience and intelligence are inseparable.

Collective Intelligence, Consciousness and Artificial Intelligence

The term 'artificial intelligence' originates from the seminal 'Dartmouth Summer Research Project on Artificial Intelligence' conference in 1956,[3] at which the founding logic of machines simulating human intelligence was formally proposed, and from which the field has since developed and grown. There are two complimentary streams of research, that of understanding and simulating human intelligence and that of developing intelligent artefacts and software. Although there are now many different conceptual and computational approaches to the simulation of human intelligence, most are founded on models of the intelligence of isolated individual animals or humans, with a significant proportion focused on the subjective first-person experience of the world or 'phenomenal consciousness'.

Many of these studies have been conducted within the closed and controlled environments of laboratories. However, all forms of life are beings that are situated within the climatic and ecological systems of the world, and all living intelligence evolved from within that context. Furthermore, it is widely acknowledged within the field of evolutionary biology that 'intelligence is manifested in social life'.[4] This 'social intelligence hypothesis' also posits that the evolution of complex societies selects for intelligence, and indeed may shape the forms and modes of intelligence that have evolved through the generations.[5] Human collective intelligence is manifested in cultural systems, and the evolution of human cultural systems reached a critical threshold of complexity more than 35,000 years ago, when long-term settlements, complex language, calendars and the material and graphical archiving of social and ecological information had fully emerged.[6] Humans are not solitary beings and human intelligence evolved through interactions with others, and so is as much a collective phenomenon as it is an individual one.

Social intelligence is not exclusively a property of human collectives, and there are many species that effectively construct complex social collectives with sophisticated responses to their climatic and ecological environments. Studies and models of collective intelligence, such as in the societies of insects and animals, are increasingly encountered in computer and social sciences, and have been intensively studied in the biological sciences. Where collective intelligence emerges, for example in insect societies, it is manifested in a material construction that reduces the load or stress on some aspects of their metabolic processes. The nests of social insects are dynamically responsive to changes in their internal and external environments, and this intelligent behaviour emerges from the interaction of millions of simple individuals, each with a very small set of innate behaviours or 'motor programmes' that are triggered by chemical, thermal or hygroscopic stimuli to their sensors. Individuals have differing thresholds and degrees of response to these stimuli, and so collective intelligent behaviour emerges from millions of slightly different interactions with the fluctuating internal and external material and metabolic conditions.[7]

Collective intelligence is an emergent phenomenon that arises from the interaction of individuals within a group, when the individuals are comparatively simple. This field of study originates from more than a century ago in William Morton Wheeler's seminal studies of the ant colony, in which he described the collective of individuals as being indistinguishable from a single organism. Wheeler used the term 'superorganism' to describe the colony, and argued that the higher-order properties could not be deduced from the properties of individual ants.[8] So, it can be said that intelligence is not just the property of a singular brain, but is situated and socially constructed, and emerges from the interaction of large numbers of relatively simpler individuals within fluctuating dynamical contexts. This suggests that collective intelligence is the appropriate model of intelligence for the integration of the systems of the intelligent city. The question therefore arises: Is consciousness necessary for a city to be intelligent, and if so does it need to resemble biological consciousness?

Recent studies of the design of complex systems in the field of artificial intelligence that are focused on the control of dynamical infrastructural systems such as large-scale web-based information services and electrical grids that cross several country borders, suggest that artificial consciousness within these systems offers increased robustness and dependability,[9] and self-regulation and integrated corrections of fluctuations under dynamic load conditions where local decisions in the decentralised grid may be contradictory with the system processes at the global level. Intelligent electrical grids, so-called 'smart grids', with bidirectional flows of both electricity and information, and multiple distributed generators of differing capacities, will need active controls in real time, and are likely to be the first implementation of intelligent systems with artificial consciousness. The US Department of Energy defines the 'smart grid' system as:

> A fully automated power delivery network that monitors and controls every customer and node, ensuring a two-way flow of electricity and information between the power plant and the appliance, and all points in between. Its distributed intelligence, coupled with broadband communications and automated control systems, enables real-time market transactions and seamless interfaces among people, buildings, industrial plants, generation facilities, and the electric network.[10]

It is clear that other infrastructural systems, including transportation, water and informational networks, have similar complexity of flows and are also converging on consciousness in artificial intelligence for their control systems.

The integration of subsidiary systems in biological intelligence is usually characterised as consciousness, both in individuals and in societies. The term 'consciousness' has such a broad usage with multiple and often conflicting definitions in so many different domains and contexts that a singular meaning is elusive. Nonetheless, it is widely accepted that consciousness is an emergent property of living systems, and that human consciousness (and more controversially, perhaps, the consciousness of many species) involves a mental model of self, or self-awareness, that is modified by experience and memory. Complex living beings use mental models of themselves and their environments in order to predict what will happen and make decisions of how to act accordingly. 'Consciousness is the property a system has by virtue of modeling itself as having sensations and making free decisions'.[11] It has been argued that a major contributor to the difficulty of defining consciousness is 'explaining the complicated interactions between the parts of the self-model'.[12]

In answer to the question: 'Is consciousness necessary for a city to be intelligent?' it can be said that machine consciousness is rapidly developing within very large infrastructural systems, and that it has some features in common with collective intelligence. Furthermore, if the city holds an internal model of itself, is aware of the processes and fluxes of its systems, and the sensory data of the flows and morphology of those systems is registered in that model, and if that self-representation has relations to models of the external environment in which it is situated, then some degree of conscious experience is enabled. A city with a higher-level intelligence would be able to use the meta-model, the self-representation situated within the model of the environment, to improve the control and regulation of its flows and to run simulations in order to predict the consequences of changes to those controls to both the city and its environment. To select between singular reactions and responses that have an immediate effectiveness and multiple sequential actions with longer-term beneficial outcomes it must be able to call on stored 'experiences' or memory of sequences of past actions and interactions, and the relative effectiveness and longer-term consequences of their implementation.

In answer to the second part of the question: 'Does it need to resemble biological consciousness?' it can be said that the consciousness of collectives is a more promising model than that of a single human being. There is progress towards defining the metrics of machine consciousness,[13] and implementation of limited 'functional consciousness' in complex software,[14] demonstrating the interaction of selective attention, working memory and decision-making. In robotics there are also advances in terms of the cognitive characteristics associated with biological consciousness.[15] Although there is as yet no concentrated research in the sciences of artificial intelligence that is directed to the specific requirements for the development of intelligent cities, it is possible to delineate a conceptual schema with a hierarchical scale of cognition

that correlates with the historic and future evolution of cities. These cognitive categories are, in ascending order of complexity: situated, reactive/responsive, adaptive/attentional and self-aware.

As illustrated here, the research agenda of the Emergent Technologies and Design (EmTech) programme at the Architectural Association (AA) in London studies cities within the first three categories, abstracting principles and parameters that are used to generate computational evolution of new city tissues that contribute to the architectural development of future cities. The 'self-aware city' does not yet exist.

The Situated City

Cities that have evolved over time are a manifestation of collective human intelligence applied episodically over thousands of years. Those that have survived evolved within regional-scale climatic and ecological systems, and are usually exceptionally well suited to climate. As regional-scale cultures co-evolved with the development of cities, the spatial values and urban behaviour of their citizens is encoded in the patterns of their streets, public spaces and buildings. The most intensively studied are the evolved cities in hot arid regions, including Yadz in Iran, Shibam in Yemen and parts of the older tissues of Fez in Morocco and Cairo in Egypt, as these are the most strongly correlated to their environmental contexts and have urban patterns that encode the spatial values of the culture.

There is a gradient in the latitudinal distribution of plant and animal species from the pole to the equator, with greater number of species occurring in the lower latitudes. It is a spatial pattern that is consistent across space, scale, marine and land habitats and all major taxonomic groups.[16] There are competing hypotheses as to how the diversity gradient may have evolved, but there is evidence to show that warmer climates have dominated much of evolutionary history and over much larger surface areas than cold climates, with corresponding faster rates of speciation. The majority of the world's cities are also in the lower latitudes, suggesting that there is a strong correlation between the spatial distribution pattern of cities and living species diversity across the face of the earth. Cities are inextricably entwined with their climatic and ecological context, and their size distribution pattern also reflects the fundamental properties of flow through networks.[17] The complexity of the relations of cities to climatic and ecological contexts is accordingly accelerated, and the sensitivity of each to changes in the other is increased.

At EmTech, Yasaman Mousavi and Fatemeh Nasseri have abstracted the physics of urban microclimates from selected vernacular morphologies and employ these principles to drive the evolution of new morphologies. These new morphologies, generated by genetic algorithms with embedded environmental analysis, are suitable for current patterns of living in high-density demographics and culturally appropriate spatial and social programmes within the context of future cities in hot arid climates.

Public Privacy Degree

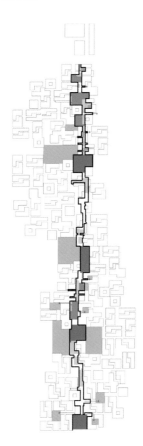

Yasaman Mousavi and Fatemeh
Nasseri, The Situated City, AA
Emergent Technologies and
Design (EmTech), Architectural
Association, London, 2010–12

There is a direct relationship between
the morphology of the city – its street
patterns, buildings and public spaces
– and the inherited spatial culture
of its inhabitants that evolved in the
context of ecological and cultural
systems. In these experiments, genetic
algorithms are used to generate
new urban morphologies that couple
environmental analysis to spatial
patterns and social programmes that
are abstracted from sample tissues of
vernacular cities.

Patch Re-informing
Route at Ground Level

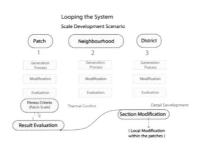

Looping the System

Scale Development Scenario

Area: 2769 m²
Total solar radiation: 4402528 wh
Average solar radiation: 1589 wh/m²

Area:3015 m²
Tsolar radiation: 7059297 wh
Average solar radiation: 2341 wh/m²

Drastic Increase in
Pedestrian thermal Comfort

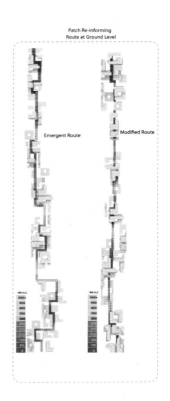

Emergent Route

Modified Route

Neighbourhood generation	Modification Strategy		Implications	Generation	Evaluation		Selection
Public Area	Patch Aggregation	Pubic area Configuration		Numeric outcome	Fitness criteria (1)	Fitness criteria (2)	
				Morphological outcome	Route distribution	Density	

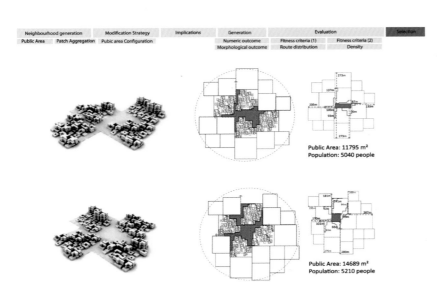

Public Area: 11795 m²
Population: 5040 people

Public Area: 14689 m²
Population: 5210 people

Elif Erdine, Population and Population Density of Cities within the Lower Latitudes, AA Emergent Technologies and Design (EmTech), Architectural Association, London, 2013

The distribution of biological species diversity is greatest in the warmer climates of the lower latitudes. A preliminary mapping of the world's 800 most populous cities suggests that the majority of the world's highly populated cities also exist within the lower latitudes.

The reactive and responsive city is situated, and in addition has sentience, the ability to sense critical changes in the flows of the external environment and within itself, and to respond by modifying or changing some aspects of the behaviour of its own systems appropriately.

The Reactive/Responsive City

The reactive and responsive city is situated, and in addition has sentience, the ability to sense critical changes in the flows of the external environment and within itself, and to respond by modifying or changing some aspects of the behaviour of its own systems appropriately. The most intensively studied are historical extended city systems that had responsive hydrological systems, such as Angkor Wat in Cambodia, and contemporary systems including the polder cities of the Netherlands.

A significant fraction of all cities are located on coastlines, at the mouths of large river deltas, in river basins and along river valleys, and all are embedded in complex hydrological flow regimes. Although many cities have been able to ameliorate decoupling from their local ecological systems by globally extending their networks for food, energy and material flows, they are always dependent on their local and regional context for water – and for the redistribution of flows generated by the city itself, including a variety of emissions and wastes.

Yu Chen and Qianqian Yu have thus proposed an experimental city located on the Mekong River, with a 6-metre (20-foot) difference in water level between the wet and dry season, which can collect and hold water within its urban blocks in the wet season and release it gradually over the dry season to irrigate crops. A complex and differentiated urban morphology is organised by urban networks that integrate residential blocks with public facilities and differing street networks and pathways for wet and dry seasons. The patterns of the river flow dynamics are used to distribute the city morphology and the agricultural territories appropriately on the contours of the basin. The morphology is fixed, but has differing patterns of usage as the water levels change, and the water systems of the city react and respond to changes in rainfall, river flows, and to agricultural demands that are constrained by groundwater levels and the temperature and humidity of the regional climate.

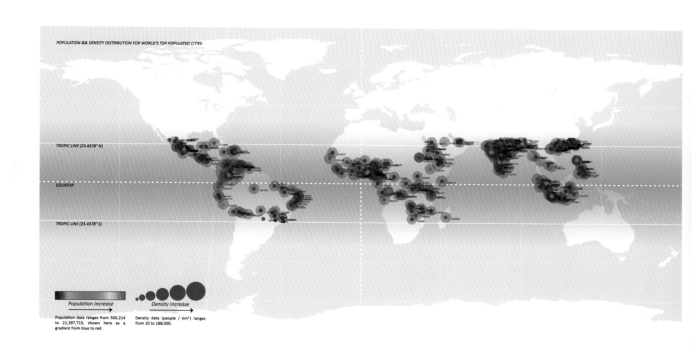

POPULATION && DENSITY DISTRIBUTION FOR WORLD'S TOP POPULATED CITIES

TROPIC LINE (23.4378° N)

EQUATOR

TROPIC LINE (23.4378° S)

Population Increase

Density Increase

Population data ranges from 500,214 to 21,397,715, shown here as a gradient from blue to red.

Density data (people / km²) ranges from 10 to 188,000.

Yu Chen and Qianqian Yu, The Reactive/Responsive City, AA Emergent Technologies and Design (EmTech), Architectural Association, London, 2009–11

Many cities are in complex hydrological flow regimes. Genetic algorithms are used to generate a new urban tissue that aggregates urban blocks hybridised with ponds and polders to hold water and release it in the dry season for agriculture. The city has the ability to sense and respond to critical changes in water levels, enabling ecological remediation and water distribution of agricultural territories.

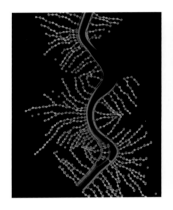

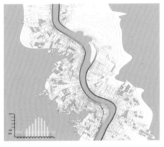

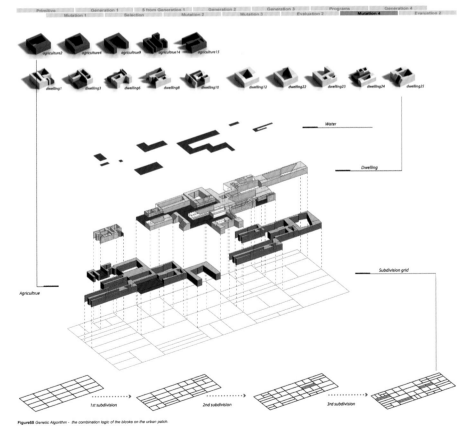

Figure55 Genetic Algorithm - the combination logic of the blocks on the urban patch.

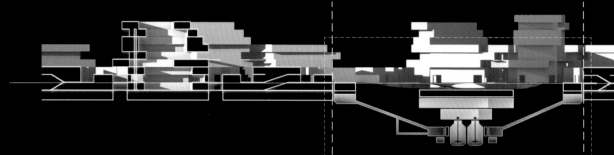

Processing Plant Cross-Section

| Underground Processing Plant

| Ground Floor Plan
- vehicular pathways junction
- spaces for waste collection
- anaerobic digestion (tonnage = 1,800 t / year)

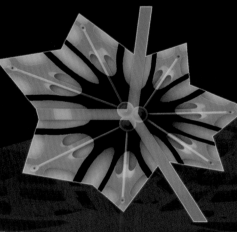

| Top View
- pedestrian pathways junction
- urban park

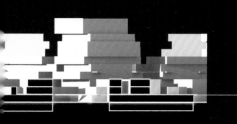

The adaptive and attentional city is situated and responsive, and in addition has the capacity to selectively change some aspects of both the behaviour and configuration of any of its infrastructural systems. It requires the capacity for selective attention to moderate changes that are beneficial at a local scale but potentially conflict with global system parameters. The most intensively studied systems are energy systems such as the 'smart grid' proposed by the US Department of Energy.

Lemire Abdul Halim Chehab and Mohamad Makkouk, The Adaptive and Attentional City, AA Emergent Technologies and Design (EmTech), Architectural Association, London, 2011–13

below and previous spread: Algorithms are here used to generate emergent morphologies of dense urban systems that have multiple pathways and movement systems embedded within them. The tissue is optimised for passive energy consumption and has the capacity to capture and distribute energy (from anaerobic digestion and photovoltaics). Energy sources can be combined or differentially weighted relative to variations in the climatic conditions and energy consumption over the different seasons.

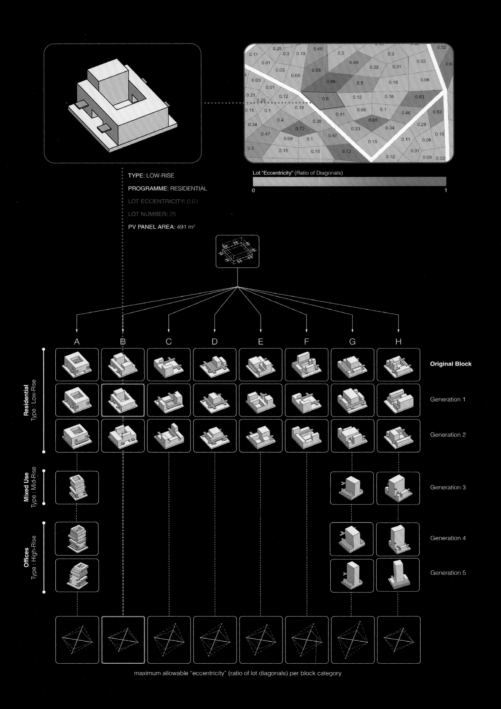

TYPE: LOW-RISE

PROGRAMME: RESIDENTIAL

LOT ECCENTRICITY: 0.61

LOT NUMBER: 25

PV PANEL AREA: 491 m²

Lot "Eccentricity" (Ratio of Diagonals)

0   1

maximum allowable "eccentricity" (ratio of lot diagonals) per block category

Original Block

Generation 1

Generation 2

Generation 3

Generation 4

Generation 5

Residential
Type : Low-Rise

Mixed Use
Type : Mid-Rise

Offices
Type : High-Rise

The Adaptive/Attentional City

The adaptive and attentional city is situated and responsive, and in addition has the capacity to selectively change some aspects of both the behaviour and configuration of any of its infrastructural systems. It requires the capacity for selective attention to moderate changes that are beneficial at a local scale but potentially conflict with global system parameters. The most intensively studied systems are energy systems such as the 'smart grid' proposed by the US Department of Energy.

Although the adaptive/attentional city does not yet exist in totality, many of the sensing instruments and technologies do, and are beginning to be deployed within separate systems. The cognitive development of the attentional city requires informational communications protocols and software systems to integrate the data from sentient systems, and the development of machine consciousness of sufficient cognitive capacity to achieve differential and selective attention.

Lemire Abdul Halim Chehab and Mohamad Makkouk propose an urban system in which two types of microscale energy sources (anaerobic digestion and photovoltaics) are embedded and distributed within the urban fabric at the scale of a dense and compact neighbourhood. Algorithms have been developed to run multiple growth simulations of the system, and optimise for differing cultural and climatic contexts. Energy sources can be switched, combined or differentially weighted in relation to urban blocks evolved and orientated for shading and passive energy strategies in differing contexts.

The Self-Aware City

The self-aware city is fully intelligent. It is 'conscious' of its citizens and the interrelation between all of its infrastructural systems, and able to synchronise its city systems with climatic and ecological effects at the regional scale. It is able to select between singular reactions and responses that have an immediate effect and multiple sequential actions, and has the capacity to learn from experiences, and to run simulations to predict the effectiveness and long-term consequences of system modifications and reconfigurations. Its spatial patterns are culturally appropriate and it is capable of planning its further expansions or contractions according to the fluctuations of its global and regional contexts. This city has yet to be achieved, but is the ultimate goal.

The Intelligent City

The concept of the intelligent city has emerged from disparate but convergent fields over the last half century, and in the last decade has become the collective endeavour that is central to the future of humans in a regime of rapidly accelerating population growth and declining resources, climatic and ecological change, and accelerating complexity of the global system. The conceptual schemata set out here are preliminary, but delineate a taxonomy with a hierarchical scale of cognition that has the potential to correlate the inherited spatial values of city cultures that are climatically located within the future evolution of cities to become 'intelligent'. ∆

NOTES
1. Michael Weinstock, 'The Evolutionary Dynamics of Sentience in Cities', in Pia Ednie-Brown, Mark Burry and Andrew Burrow (eds), ∆ *The Innovation Imperative: Architectures of Vitality*, Jan/Feb (no 1) 2013, pp 92–7.
2. The scientific study of the city and its systems is now a rapidly expanding domain that cuts across so many disciplinary and professional boundaries that it is impossible to provide a definitive list of all who take a scientific approach to their studies. It includes, among many others, complexity scientists, urban physicists and climatologists, economists and ecologists, systems and civil engineers, software and information/data specialists, artificial intelligence designers and, increasingly, architects and urbanists.
3. The founding logic of the 'Dartmouth Conference' and John McCarthy, Marvin Minsky, Nathaniel Rochester and Claude Shannon's proposal for a 'Research Project on Artificial Intelligence' was that 'all aspects of intelligence can be so accurately described that a machine can be made to simulate it'. See J McCarthy, M Minsky, N Rochester and C Shannon, 'A Proposal for the Dartmouth Summer Research Project on Artificial Intelligence', 1955, archived in Dartmouth College, New Hampshire.
4. Richard Byrne and Andrew Whiten, 'Taking Machiavellian Intelligence Apart', *Machiavellian Intelligence: Social Complexity and the Evolution of Intellect in Monkeys, Apes and Humans*, Oxford University Press (Oxford), 1988, pp 50–65, and Andrew Whiten and Carel P van Schaik, 'The Evolution of Animal Cultures and Social Intelligence', *Philosophical Transactions of the Royal Society B* 362, 2007, pp 603–20.
5. Simon Reader, Yike Hager and Kevin Laland, 'The Evolution of Primate General and Cultural Intelligence', *Philosophical Transactions of the Royal Society B* 366, 2011, pp 1017–27.
6. Michael Weinstock, 'Humans: Anatomical and Cultural Forms', *The Architecture of Emergence: The Evolution of Form in Nature and Civilisation*, John Wiley & Sons (Chichester), 2010, pp 146–75.
7. Guy Theraulaz, Jacques Gautrais, Scott Camazine and Jean-Louis Deneubourg, 'The Formation of Spatial Patterns in Social Insects: From Simple Behaviours to Complex Structures', *Philosophical Transactions of the Royal Society A* 361(1807): *Self-Organization: The Quest for the Origin and Evolution of Structure*, 2003, pp 1263–82.

8. See William Morton Wheeler, 'The Ant Colony as an Organism', *Journal of Morphology* 22(2), 1911, pp 307–25; 'Emergent Evolution and the Social', *Science* 64(1662), 1926, pp 433–40; and *The Social Insects: Their Origin and Evolution*, Kegan Paul, Trench, Trubner (London), 1928.
9. Ricardo Sanz, Ignatio López and Julita Bermejo-Alonso, 'A Rationale and Vision for Machine Consciousness in Complex Controllers', in Antonio Chella and Riccardo Manzotti (eds), *Artificial Consciousness*, Imprint Academic (Exeter), 2007, pp 141–55.
10. US Department of Energy, 'Grid 2030: A National Vision for Electricity's Second 100 Years', Technical Report, 2003.
11. Drew McDermott, 'Artificial Intelligence and Consciousness', in Philip David Zelazo, Morris Moscovitch and Evan Thompson (eds), *The Cambridge Handbook of Consciousness*, Cambridge University Press (Cambridge), 2007, pp 117–50.
12. Marvin Minsky, 'Matter, Mind and Models', in *Proceedings of the International Federation of Information Processing Congress*, Vol 1, 1965, pp 45–9.
13. Raul Arrabales, Agapito Ledezma and Araceli Sanchis, 'Establishing a Roadmap and Metrics for Conscious Machines Development', *8th IEEE International Conference on Cognitive Informatics*, IEEE, 2009, pp 94–101.
14. Stan Franklin, 'IDA: A Conscious Artifact?', *Journal of Consciousness Studies*, 2009, pp 47–66.
15. David Gamez, 'Progress in Machine Consciousness', *Journal of Consciousness and Cognition* 17(3), 2008, pp 887–910.
16. Helmut Hillebrand, 'On the Generality of the Latitudinal Diversity Gradient', *The American Naturalist* 163, 2004, pp 192–211.
17. Ethan Decker, Andrew Kerkhoff and Melanie Moses, 'Global Patterns of City Size Distributions and their Fundamental Drivers', *PLOS ONE* 2(9):e934, 2007.

DARWIN
AMONG
THE
MACHINE

Tokyo Bay street light network
Tokyo Bay has a population of approximately
22 million, connected by a highly integrated
technological network. The human brain consists of
1×10^{16} neurons, providing Tokyo Bay with a neural
network of 2.2×10^{23}.

In the mid-19th century, Samuel Butler in his article 'Darwin among the Machines' provided a theory for the iterative development of machines over time. Here, London-based architect, theorist, editor and writer **Jack Self** casts 'the modern city' as 'a multiplex superposition of network infrastructures', defined by hierarchical systems of information and material exchange. He argues that current informational technologies have the power to conversely hyper-centralise or hyper-localise the city, thus either encouraging disengagement or nurturing engagement with the emergent social practices of the city's inhabitants.

Jack Self

In 1863, four years after Charles Darwin published *On the Origin of Species*, a New Zealand author named Samuel Butler reframed the idea of natural selection as a purely mechanical process. He believed nature was a colossal engine producing unlimited variations based on complex, but comprehensible, rules. In his article titled 'Darwin among the Machines' (1863),[1] he argued that the adaptation of species by incremental augmentation is no different from tools that are progressively improved by selection and refinement. He speculated that if reproduction was thought of as a form of functional adaptation, one might invert the comparison and suggest that machines themselves undergo an evolutionary process. What he put forward was both a theory for the iterative development of machines throughout history, and also – with remarkable imagination – a vision of the future in which self-regulating automatons surpass, enslave and exterminate the human race.

Butler's dual assertion that nature is machine-like, and therefore that machines conform to natural laws, became an enormously influential metaphor. It was only with the secularisation of science at the end of the 19th century that the true implications of the comparison became apparent. Up until this point science in general, and particularly the natural sciences like botany, had set the human subject apart. This is because belief in God guaranteed the existence of a human soul, which afforded us a privileged position in the world. Even sceptics, like the Deists with their blind demiurge, admitted the probability of a 'ghost in the shell' – some ethereal *anima* propping up our corpses. But without absolute belief underwriting existence, the organic-machine metaphor stepped in to explain away notions like the soul as simulations of gestalt. It proposed that all organisms, including human beings, were merely bundles of biological systems – vast accumulations of reproductive processes and regulating mechanisms that ranged from the molecular, chemical and mitochondrial to the vascular, hormonal and alimentary. It described the mysterious products of these systems (such as our psychology or personalities) as essentially emergent properties.

The simplicity of the metaphor is attractive, but herein lies the danger. By rationalising intelligence and placing it on a sliding scale with technological complexity, it flattens the notion of emergence. Consequently, it leads to much confusion about what the term actually means – architects frequently, and erroneously, categorise phenomena as emergent when they are simply describing complex non-hierarchical networks. Indeed, even when the system in question does display emergent qualities, that does not mean it is forcibly displaying any form of 'intelligent' behaviour. In a philosophical, or even a botanical sense, emergent properties are products of inexplicable causes, and fundamentally irreducible. Accordingly, intelligence transcends analysis as merely the sum of biological functions, even though it is forcibly the product of them.

Just because the Internet has the synaptic equivalent of 1,000 human brains[2] does not mean it has a capacity for conscious thought. That is, its emergent properties are not ones related to reason, which unfortunately Butler's metaphor fails to identify. The neurological architecture of the human brain evolved over several hundred millennia. It is difficult to imagine that a machine built in just 20 years (and for radically different purposes) could develop a 'mind' in any meaningful sense of the term, either now or in the future.

Butler's metaphor correctly describes organisms as both complete units and agglomerations of fluctuating systems, but unfortunately it also conflates complexity with emergence.

Nike+ City Runs
The Nike+ City Runs social media application tracks, records and maps all running routes throughout Manhattan, giving unique readings of the social and spatial urban environment.

LAT: 40.73342
LON: -73.97659

distance: 0.2 miles
time: 02m.43s

What's in a Name?

To understand human psychology as emergent is not to say it is totally incomprehensible. But it is mysterious: after all, what man could claim to know his own mind? Its motivations and operations remain impenetrable; therefore its replication is unfeasible and its simulation is impossible. Accordingly, attempts to model human agents in emergent systems are at best simplistic, and more likely misleading. This is partly because of insufficiently sophisticated computers, which necessitate a high degree of abstraction in order to execute models. However, more critically it is an epistemological problem of access. The vast range of unknown factors contributing to the complexity of high-order emergent systems remains conceptually (as well as technologically) out of reach.

Butler's metaphor correctly describes organisms as both complete units and agglomerations of fluctuating systems, but unfortunately it also conflates complexity with emergence. At the urban scale, the ramification of extrapolating this idea is that designers tend to view the city as an emergent living entity with an almost anthropomorphic personality. More properly, the modern city is a multiplex superposition of network infrastructures – but these networks, no matter how elaborate, are neither intelligent nor emergent. Historically, cities have always been defined by hierarchical systems of information and material exchange. These mechanisms exist in order to govern and exploit atomic units (buildings, traditionally residences) for the benefit of whosoever administers the urban population. In other words, cities are defined by centralised infrastructure operated for profit. This is true for the Roman aqueducts, which were made possible only by the systematic naming of streets and households (in order to tax the supply of water), and it is also true today. Great cities like London only exist because of the civic works that provide them with water, sewerage and gas. The incremental evolution of the urban realm is necessarily a narrative of its infrastructural progress: the postal service, electricity, telephone, the Internet, public transport, etc. In the sense that each new urban technology describes a tributary distribution of resources ending in a unit, the city must be 'digitised' – from the Latin word for finger, which rather aptly denotes both an integer and an extremity. The digitisation of a built landscape is essentially one of identification and naming. And like the successive strata of resources, digitisation also becomes more complex over time as precise information about the beneficiary of the services becomes more significant. Street

names, house numbers, postcodes, and IP addresses all form part of an informatic chain. First each building, and ultimately each individual, must be readily identifiable.

Philosophers like Michel Foucault have presented this process as the dystopian evolution of surveillance and control; certainly this forms an important aspect, although this factor is subservient to the primary concern of the state and corporation – the monetisation of the citizen. Over centuries, the value of a building as a physical construction has become replaced with its value in relation to a complex branching network of services (one need only consider how proximity to metro stations influences property prices). Since most of these services are subterranean (if not initially, then ultimately), the nodal city is comparable to a vast forest with interconnected roots. And like a forest, while no individual building is very old, the traces, if not the infrastructure itself, can be very ancient indeed.

Emergence and Urban Infrastructure

To understand how contemporary technologies are changing our use of urban space we must make a clear separation between those that reinforce the tributary nature of cities and those that augment the emergent social practices of the city's inhabitants. The dyadic tension between these two types of infrastructure is fundamentally the privatisation of urban space versus the democratisation of urban space. On the one hand, service companies are removing the necessity for the individual to engage in communal activities (one can well imagine a comparable argument being that the introduction of running water killed the vibrant social life surrounding city wells). And on the other hand, emergent technologies are liberating the citizen to engage with public space in new and often startling ways.

Map of Twitter vs Flickr users
Mapping Twitter and Flickr users in London (left), New York (opposite top left) and São Paulo (opposite bottom left) reveals the vast and complex networks of information generated and shared within these cities, allowing users to engage with the urban environment in new ways.

Notwithstanding our historical relationship with patronage and commercial interests, architects and designers have a responsibility to improve the civic domain of our cities.

The somewhat paradoxical paradigm underpinning the 21st-century city is a process of corporate hyper-centralisation while its inhabitants are moving towards hyper-localisation. Companies like Amazon, or services like home delivery of online grocery shopping, piggyback on existing infrastructures – they contribute to the digitisation of the home unit by further removing the necessity of the recipient to leave their building. These are not the same as infrastructures that elevate the complexity of human agency in their causal chain of action. These human-based infrastructures execute spatial and social tasks by employing different combinations of technologies, making them irreducible to the properties of any single component.

A prime example of this would be the rising popularity of online car clubs. Zipcar allows users to share vehicles, and it integrates diverse Internet protocols (online bank accounts and time-management rosters) with cellular networks, RFID chips and GPS positioning. The emergent product of these, which could not easily be predicted from any one technology, is the democratisation of vehicular access for the metropolitan populace. It turns the ultimate private realm, the car, into a piece of public infrastructure. And the impact on urban space is drastic: fewer car parks, quieter streets, cleaner air, more efficient management of resources and risks.

Even in this one domain, the trajectory is far from complete: a young American company called Panda Park fragments the process even further, allowing suburbanites to hire out their own cars to their direct neighbours. The firm has been a vocal petitioner in California for legalising driverless cars, which when it happens will make the shared auto-network even more fluid and responsive. What makes these companies unlike Amazon is that their modus operandi is primarily social, and they rely heavily on user-generated content and maintenance. Basically, while Amazon employs complex algorithms to simulate work that in another era would have been done by humans, companies like Zipcar are using dispersed networks of actual human agents to achieve their complexity.

Notwithstanding our historical relationship with patronage and commercial interests, architects and designers have a responsibility to improve the civic domain of our cities. We therefore have two possible courses of action in this condition: either as agents of Darwinian selection, curbing the dangerous mutations that exacerbate the commercialisation of the public realm. Or we can position ourselves as urban experimenters, speculators and technological developers, promoting mutations that harness the awesome power of laterally connected individuals for the transformation of urban space. ⌀

Notes
1. Samuel Butler, 'Darwin Among the Machines', first published in *The Press* newspaper, 13 June 1863.
2. The Internet has been estimated to contain about 10^{18} transistors. By comparison, the average human brain has a neural count of around 10^{16}.

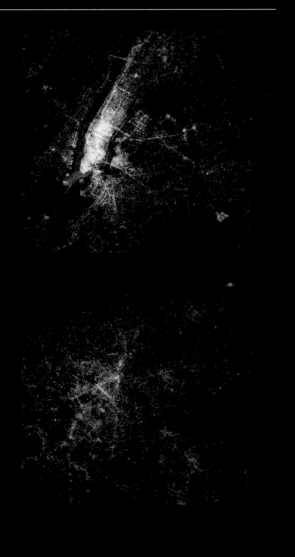

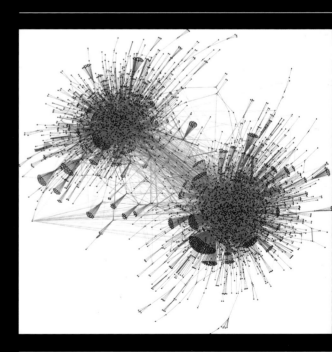

Dynamic network of Twitter users using the #gop tag
While specific topics discussed on Twitter and other social media sites may begin as local or regional conversations, the networks generated describe larger infrastructural systems connecting inhabitants of the city and beyond.

Joan Busquets

CITIES AND GRIDS
IN SEARCH OF NEW PARADIGMS

**Joan Busquets, Manhattan Grid, New York,
Manhattan Grid Studio, Harvard Graduate School of
Design (GSD), Cambridge, Massachusetts, 2012**
Manhattan employs an asymmetrical grid superimposed
on an irregular topography. Developed in the 19th century,
this grid is a good example of how the generation of
regular plot sizes and repetitive geometries shaped the
way in which the city is used and perceived.

The wider global influences of expanded populations, new technologies and economies in both Europe and the Far East are having a direct impact on the pattern and planning of urban form. **Joan Busquets**, the principal of B Arquitectura I Urbanisme (BAU) in Barcelona, and Professor in Practice of Urban Planning and Design at Harvard Graduate School of Design (GSD), describes how the urban grid is continuing to evolve with these changes, becoming 'a matrix for innovation within urban development, allowing the creation of sustainable and compact cities', enabling the forming of 'new networks and innovative city systems'.

In order to meet the demands of the new urban conditions that are resulting from expanded populations, new technologies and economies in both Europe and the Far East, postwar urban planning models are now being reviewed, and it is to be expected that consequential reconfigurations and new paradigms may emerge. The industrial system that induced much of the urbanisation of the Western world now plays a secondary role, and today new dynamics operate both in urban centres and in the surrounding areas of influence, which in turn generate new and highly innovative metropolitan conditions. In response to these new economic dynamics and the demands of emerging urban culture, a transformation in the forms and the processes of city design is now taking place.

The publication *X Lines: A New Lens for the Urbanistic Project,*[1] edited with Felipe Correa, presents a number of models and paradigms used in recent city design, outlining as many as 10 different approaches with no single dominant or exclusive form. The aim was to emphasise the value of reconsidering open forms for city design, in parallel with the 'Revisiting the Urban Grid' research underway at the Harvard Graduate School of Design (GSD) since 2008.

The presence of regular forms or grids is manifest in the design of cities and their extension into conurbations. Some are almost automatic processes of decomposition of the land and infrastructures for subsequent construction in interstitial spaces, tending to produce a rather banal city, or a 'city without attributes'.[2] Others, however, offer potential for innovation in city design because they ensure basic urban coherence, at the same time allowing a high degree of versatility over time. Like score sheets on which multiple forms of music can be written, these new grids are the reference models that new research into urban planning takes as its departure point. In order to explore the new conditions of current urban forms in accordance with the culture of the sustainable city now so forcefully emerging, and to find a method to enhance the complex process of city design, it is necessary to examine the qualities and physical conditions of grids in the development of the contemporary city.

The Qualities of Grid-Plan Cities

In recent years it is the geometrically regular city that has been synonymous with urban plans, as opposed to the organic plans of more rural arrangements. The former appears to be the most persistent of anthropological systems for organising collective life – its geometric order allows for differentiation with equality, although in some cultures it also enables what American surveyor John Randel Jr said of Manhattan, the facilitation of 'buying, selling and improving real estate'.[3] The development of the grid-plan city over time is a significant index of human societies and their urban history, from the first planned cities in ancient history that were organised as grid systems through the evolution of the general design of the grid and the specific characteristics of its application: from the ancient Asian models consisting of a city of aristocrats and tradesmen built around a palace and oriental variations, re-adopted in Greece, to the organisation of Roman military camps and territory, to the bastions built to control the countryside in medieval Europe.

During the Renaissance, the formalisation of the regular city ideal, with its fortifications, served above all as an instrument of war and provided precedents that were adapted for the foundation of cities in the New World. The cities of the Enlightenment produced brilliant episodes in the history of urban Europe, and in the US Jefferson drafted the Land Ordinance of 1785 that imposed a regular grid of land boundaries that extended westwards across the continent regardless of the natural features of the topography, with one-mile-square plot divisions that organised the territory from the Ohio River to the western seaboard within which the city was a medium-scale consequence.

In the 19th century, the re-adoption of the grid plan in Europe for the rationalisation of the emerging industrial cities led to guidelines for the development of the modern city, as it allowed for the generation of regular plot sizes and repetitive geometries. Berlin, Barcelona and Milan in Europe, but also New York and Chicago, are clear examples. Later, these grid systems were reappraised in the development and organisation of the 20th-century city and replaced by network city planning with larger super-grid systems designed to make

and characteristics of grids vary, and the parameters guiding the dimensions and configurations are also vital to the quality of the city's future. Furthermore, while there are often common definitions of occupation and building height, uses and other municipal codes, regulations and by-laws among cities with distinct cultural contexts, their manifestation as three-dimensional forms may differ significantly.

In continuous evolution, grid-plan cities allow for transformation over time, as the grid system is generally more adaptable to the emerging requirements of changing urban societies. The process begins with occupation of the city block, on its edges or over the whole plot. Greater density emerges from the

infrastructures more efficient. However, in recent years there have been the beginnings of a return to smaller grids, as the quality of the urban spaces they generate is now seen to be at least as significant as the efficiency of the traffic flows and superblocks of larger grids.

Grid systems have been adapted over time and implemented in different cultural constructs, and their value for cities is still significant in contemporary urban design strategies. The design of city networks is generally regarded as two-dimensional, in the sense that although it primarily defines the ground plan, the form

widening of streets to allow an increase in the heights of buildings, concentrating them on the perimeter. This may be phased sequentially, coherent with the existing city, or represent a break with previous configurations and give rise to random building development that impairs the continuity of the grid. The inherent adaptability of the grid may thus lead to the disruption of the urban coherence established in the initial stages. This is the case for many American grid plans, where sudden changes in volume, often due to the introduction of skyscrapers of arbitrary height, lead to imbalances in the urban structure

Barcelona, Spain
The 'superimposed city', as exemplified by Barcelona, reduces the role of the old city centre by superimposing an innovative global grid over the traditional city.

San Francisco, California
San Francisco is an example of the 'accumulative city', where different grid geometries are developed in local patches over time.

Categories of Grid-Plan Cities

To further understand the variations of grid systems and their effects on the urban environment, we can identify six distinct categories that are defined by the formal properties of their grids and the relation of these to their neighbouring territories. In the 'accumulative city', different grids are developed and juxtaposed over time. This type of city has frequently occurred throughout history, commonly having separate and distinct sectors, as in the case of Turin, Montreal, San Francisco and Saint Petersburg, in which the successions of grids have been added together to form coherent, well-organised wholes. The 'superimposed city' consists of an innovative

that are detrimental to the value of the city block as an entity. However, in some cases, such as Manhattan, such height increases have largely maintained the order and continuity of the block, resulting in a new definition of the urban project.

Some city grids, such as many of the original chequerboard layouts in Latin America, are based on a sequence of blocks and streets, while others are the product of predominant infrastructures such as highways, railways and elevated or subterranean transit systems. Some, such as New York or Barcelona, judiciously combine the two systems: streets and avenues constitute the grid, while the infrastructure and land itself shape the supporting framework. The advantage of this layout is that it produces efficient cities with a

high degree of urbanity. Recent research on the development of Manhattan from 1811 to 2011 shows how the application of the original grid was adapted to the island's irregular topography, and reveals the capacity of this asymmetrical rectangular grid to incorporate the changes over the last two centuries. By contrast, the major transformations of its riverfronts are less coherent with the logic of the seminal grid, and this is where new design paradigms are needed. How might a reinterpretation of the grid serve to integrate Manhattan's new waterfronts with its interior?

grid superimposed on a traditional city, planned as a large extension and resulting in the reduction of the role of the old centre. Very different examples of this are the ancient Greek city of Miletus, Mexico City, New York, Barcelona and Milan.

The 'discontinuous city' variant has separate sectors or fragments characterised by different grid systems, each designed to meet the needs of specific programmes, thus creating individual neighbourhoods with particular identities, but rarely combined into a coherent whole. Trieste, Lisbon, Edinburgh and

Algiers, Algeria
Algiers can be categorised as a 'discontinuous city', where neighbourhoods with specific identities develop as a result of the combination of individual grid forms.

Los Angeles, California
'Infinite cities' like Los Angeles have uninterrupted extensions of their original grids.

Algiers are examples of this category. The 'infinite city' is defined by the uninterrupted extension of the foundational grid. Grid systems such as this are often found in Latin American cities, for example Santiago de Chile and Buenos Aires, both of which were founded after the New Laws of the Indies were passed in 1542, and also in North American cities, including Los Angeles.

In the 'cellular city', multiple complex cells are aggregated to form a continuous whole. The unit cell is not a singular block endlessly repeated, as in the infinite city, but rather a group of blocks organised into a cluster that is repetitively deployed. Savannah, Islamabad, Brasilia and Milton Keynes are all cellular cities. The sixth classification of grid-system cities is the 'city of different scales'. Cities within this category, such

as Houston, Seoul and Chandigarh, have a clear hierarchal system in their networks of streets and avenues, and were greatly influenced by the regulation of traffic and public transport that was so dominant in the second half of the 20th century.

Grid systems have significant potential in the design of the high-density cities that demographic changes and emergent economies are demanding, and an examination of the historical evolution and diversity of grid systems offers valuable insights for the development of new paradigms. Chicago is a good example

of how the influence of both the urban grid and Jefferson's territorial grid have enabled the integration of the city's canal system with its larger infrastructural networks. The result is a city in which mixed uses and density are strong features, and where a diversity of architecture and changes in programme are easily accommodated.

The Gallery of Gridded Cities
The 'Gallery of Gridded Cities' (part of the Harvard GSD 'Revisiting the Urban Grid' research project) was featured at the 'Cerdà and the Barcelona of the Future' exhibition at the Centre de Cultura Contemporània de Barcelona (CCCB) in 2009 and presented analyses of urban projects that varied greatly in scale, content and ambition. Some

responded to an overall city project, such as those for Manhattan and Barcelona, or set out to produce large city fragments that followed the order imposed by the existing grid but had a high degree of autonomy. Others were grid systems used as mechanisms of administrative and political control for large regions or countries, as in the cases of Rome or the US.

In the 21st century, it seems that though grid systems continue to be employed at these three levels, they are capable of accommodating so much more. New paradigms might comprise multiple layers that act both

Milton Keynes, Buckinghamshire, UK
above: Milton Keynes was developed as a 'cellular city', where multiple complex cells are aggregated to form a continuous whole.

Seoul, South Korea
above: Seoul is an example of a 'city on different scales', a design based on transportation networks infilled with city blocks.

at territorial and urban scales that work with large flow infrastructures such as railways and motorways, and finer capillary networks, and can create spatial systems at a variety of scales. Zaha Hadid's One North Masterplan, Singapore (due for completion in 2021) seeks to create a continuous urban space, the grid used to harmonise with the topography and the third dimension ensuring the project's formal continuity. Other examples are Peter Eisenman's Rebstockpark organic grids in Frankfurt (2002–) and Foster + Partners' Masdar City solid single grid in Abu Dhabi (2007–).

Currently under construction, these are projects that prompt further examination of other, less obvious dimensions of cities that can enhance the use of grids in urban design

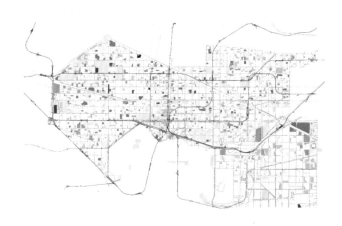

and respond more efficiently to new urban cultures. The grid can be an efficient device for defining geographical conditions, leading to the re-naturalisation of the city. In doing so, it has the ability to respect and improve environmental conditions within the city and within its natural surroundings. The city grid acts as a framework for the evolution of architecture over time, sensing the need for change as well as instrumentalising its adaptations. As a versatile mechanism, it creates change in the use of public space, and its awareness of the changing lifestyles and systems of production often caused by technological advances, provides flexibility and choice for future sustainable cities. The city must reproduce and recycle, bridging the gap between infrastructures that create

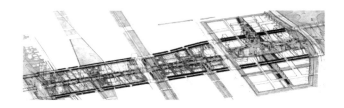

urban fragments, and developing them to enhance its qualities.

The grid is a matrix for innovation within urban development, allowing the creation of sustainable and compact cities, and the generation, continuity and connectivity of not only traditional urban infrastructures, but also green spaces, forming new networks and innovative city systems. ⊅

Notes
1. Joan Busquets and Felipe Correa, *X Lines: A New Lens for the Urbanistic Project*, Actar (Barcelona), 2006.
2. The 'city without attributes' notion of modern cities refers to Robert Musil's unfinished novel *The Man Without Qualities*, whose main character Ulrich leads a completely indifferent life. See Robert Musil, *Der Mann ohne Eigenschaften, Buch 1*, Rowohlt Verlag (Reinbeck), 1930.
3. Kenneth T Jackson, *Crabgrass Frontier: The Suburbanization of The United States*, Oxford University Press (New York), 1985, p 74.

Joan Busquets et al, Cerdà Eixample, Barcelona, 'Revisiting the Urban Grid' project, Harvard Graduate School of Design, Cambridge, Massachusetts, 2009
top: The Underground grid system. The extended network of infrastructural connections and facilities beneath the streets includes some that connect below ground into the urban blocks.

centre: Barcelona's extended grid system within which green spaces and public buildings frame a connective tissue that concentrates a high density of civic life.

B Landsape, Architecture and Urbanism (BAU), Central Civic Corridor of Eastern New Town, Ningbo, Zhejiang Province, China, 2009–12
bottom: The urban landscape strategy here uses a double system of orthogonal and oblique, a combination of geometries and scales that enables the opportunistic changes of programme as time progresses without disrupting existing flows and connections.

Eva Castro, José Alfredo Ramírez and Eduardo Rico

THE GROUNDS OF A RENEWED PRACTICE

GROUNDLAB'S APPROACH TOWARDS LANDSCAPE AND INFRASTRUCTURE

Based in London and Beijing, Groundlab is an emerging international practice that specialises in landscape urbanism. **Eva Castro, José Alfredo Ramírez and Eduardo Rico** of Groundlab describe the potential that the ground itself provides for a new urbanism, which is able to integrate multiple fields and scales while also engaging with greater territorial systems. They explain how landscape architect Frederick Law Olmsted was influential in establishing an approach that uses ecological infrastructure as the basis for design. They proceed in describing two Groundlab projects that integrate ground remediation and water infrastructure techniques: Paisajes Latentes urban design masterplan for Valle De Chalco Solidaridad in Mexico City (2011) and the Ground Ecologies masterplan for the redevelopment of the Jiading District in Shanghai (2010).

The contemporary architectural climate is saturated with generic and autonomous urban developments, devoid of public space due to market forces and political ensembles. Within the built environment, the landscape has conventionally been used for aesthetic purposes. However, Groundlab questions this role, proposing a new methodology for the creation of contemporary urbanisation capable of generating, integrating and mediating ecological systems within a greater understanding of 'ground'.[1] Exploring the potential of the ground through the employment of trans-disciplinary and performance-oriented engineering techniques, past traditional landscape remediation and problem-solving approaches, can produce an urbanism that intrinsically integrates multiple fields and scales within the design process and is engaged in larger territorial systems.

Infrastructural Landscapes

Emerging design disciplines are now beginning to consider ecological infrastructure as the basis for design concepts informing urban and architectural character. This approach stems from the work of landscape architect Frederick Law Olmsted in the mid- to late 19th century, based on the integration of engineering systems in the design of metropolitan landscapes.[2] In his seminal Emerald Necklace project, for example, in 1878 Olmsted instituted a 4.5-kilometre (2.8-mile) chain of parks along the Boston Peninsula in Massachusetts. By dredging the land from the Muddy River to the Charles River, he incorporated ecological regeneration within a park setting, integrating water infrastructure, pedestrian and social networks.[3]

Similarly, the Bronx River Parkway project, New York, initiated by landscape architects Herman Merkel and Gilmore Clarke in the 1920s, sought to continue the integration of once-separate systems by investigating how the morphology of the parkway – then a new urban typology – could be created with the automobile driver in mind. The idea developed under the engineers Leslie Holleran and Arthur Hayden, who further explored the constraints linked to driving, and employed smooth road curvatures, grade-separated junctions and other landscape design features.[4] The project proved so successful that in the early 1950s it was extended to Soundview Park, south of the Bronx, by urban planner Robert Moses, and soon became the norm for all driving routes, eventually giving way to what we know today as the motorway.

But however pioneering these infrastructural works were, the landscape principles that generated them are no longer viable in modern, highly urbanised environments. Today's cities are susceptible to high migration rates and huge developmental pressures that demand immediate responses to urban sprawl, rapid urbanisation, post-industrialisation and natural disasters via the design and implementation of integrated ecological and infrastructural systems. In this context, Groundlab works actively to propose alternative models of urbanisation: rethinking organisational structures, diagramming new urban networks, indexing sensitive territorial readings and exploring the generative potential of landscape as infrastructure, through the manipulation of the ground and its systems. Its research and built work therefore employ the ground through strategies articulating new structures and territories within specific design frameworks, and addressing their viability and pertinence within contemporary urban environments.

Employing the Ground for Ecological Remediation

Two Groundlab projects that apply ground remediation and water infrastructure techniques through an integrated systems approach are the Paisajes Latentes urban design masterplan for Valle De Chalco Solidaridad on the eastern outskirts of Mexico City (2011) and the Ground Ecologies masterplan for the redevelopment of the Jiading District, Shanghai (2010). Paisajes Latentes, developed with the AA Mexico City Visiting School at the Architectural Association, London, as part of its Recovering Waterscapes studio, is located on former agricultural land on Lake Chalco that was informally developed during the city's industrial expansion in the late 20th century. Ground Ecologies, which won first prize in the Jiading Urban Design Master Planning International Competition, is located in a post-industrial area of one of Shanghai's suburbs that is projected for gentrification due to the planned extension of the city's Metro. Both projects investigate contemporary urban conditions, such as rapid urbanisation, de-industrialisation and infrastructural deficiency, in informal settlements as design drivers for the development of ecological remediation systems and new urban morphologies.

PAISAJES LATENTES

Valle De Chalco is situated at one of the main entry points to Mexico City and connected by the Mexico-Puebla Highway, a major infrastructural facility. The cessation of agricultural production brought about by the pressure for commercially developable land, and the pollution caused by nearby industrial areas, made the municipality an ideal location for the informal settlement of workers and immigrants, which led to its rapid urbanisation in the late 20th century.

These conditions shaped, and continue to shape, Valle de Chalco's urban fabric and the way it is used by its inhabitants. It has been developed as a continuous and homogeneous urban grid that, due to its rapid and unplanned growth, lacks any public facilities for its primarily residential areas. From a social standpoint, the lack of parks, plazas and other gathering spaces has led to the use of the city's streets as its primary public network, in the form of weekly markets and other commercial enterprises. From an ecological perspective, the city's geographical location on the old bed of Lake Chalco, and its surrounding water infrastructures – including open-air wastewater canals – means it is prone to flooding, mainly during the rainy season, which fails to drain due to the poor infrastructure.

Groundlab with the AA Mexico City Visiting School, Paisajes Latentes, Valle De Chalco Solidaridad, Mexico, 2011
Mexico City's urban development has forced the gradual disappearance of its lakes as its natural ecological system, causing regular flooding and a scarcity of water along the way.

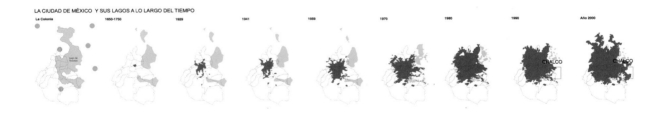

The water management strategy at Valle de Chalco is a territory-scale intervention that engages different perspectives of the city to propose an ecology that goes beyond purely environmental concerns.

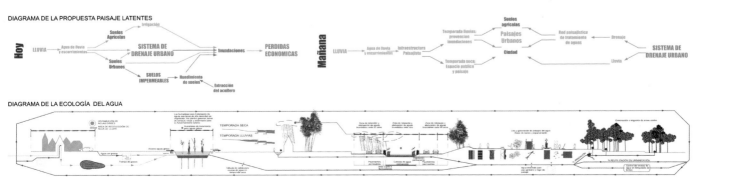

Paisajes Latentes therefore has as its focus the idea of recovering water landscapes, with the integration of social and geographical issues as design drivers. The integration of these systems stems from an understanding of Mexico City as a megalopolis intrinsically related to its geographic and ecological conditions in an endorheic, or closed drainage, basin, where water infrastructure plays a fundamental role at a territorial scale. Furthermore, the project acknowledges Valle de Chalco's street networks as the grounds from where to explore the material potentials of its own urban environment. In other words, it sees the municipality as part of a larger, natural-water and social-street territorial system with the capacity to affect the design process across different hierarchical scales. To this end, water is the system's main device, capable of sustaining, creating and organising the public realm to produce a socially infrastructured public space.

Through an understanding of Valle de Chalco's natural drainage, flood risks, existing public markets and commercial corridors, Paisajes Latentes proposes the generation of a manifold water infrastructure that acts as a spine or anchor for its social spaces. Through research, it explores the possibility of integrating landscape and engineering techniques within the design of coherent urban systems. And in doing so, it employs water management systems, water purification and earthwork strategies that become the mechanisms with which to enhance the city's social and spatial structure. The project therefore uses infrastructure as the raw material with which to articulate urban networks for the flow of transportation, communication and social exchange through the manipulation of water and ground.

This interconnectivity of public space and infrastructure results in an alternative material model of urban organisation, in which urban and environmental data on existing conditions is utilised as more than a remedial device, as in traditional predecessors, to produce a new spatial understanding of the city, its programmes and activities. By intensifying social interactions, Paisajes Latentes provides a fertile ground on which to rethink new urban configurations, and challenge current trends and existing notions of the city's public, private and semi-private spatial networks.

In this context, the street/water network as a ground condition – an artificial construct generated by simple operations derived primarily from pragmatic approaches to address technical demand – expands from a purely utilitarian state to acquire further spatial specificity. The objective, then, is to create diversity, identity and place: an urban environment capable of fostering a highly complex set of interactions among infrastructural, cultural and social conditions, fostering a synthesis of landscape infrastructure and architecture, and promoting new spatial conditions, arrangements and adjacencies.

The project [...] uses infrastructure as the raw material with which to articulate urban networks for the flow of transportation, communication and social exchange through the manipulation of water and ground.

top: In reading the natural runoff through the existing street network within Valle de Chalco the framework for the project emerges as a new spatial construct.

centre: Natural drainage, flood risks, existing public markets and commercial corridors are the basis for a manifold water infrastructure that serves as a spine, or anchor, for Valle de Chalco's social spaces.

bottom: Flood risk analysis. Indexing of the existing flood risk areas of Valle de Chalco gives an understanding of its natural ecological systems so that a new water infrastructure capable of supporting the city's social spaces can be created.

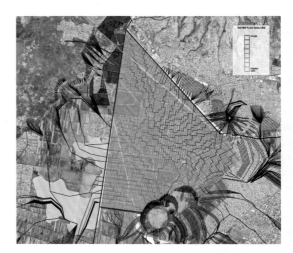

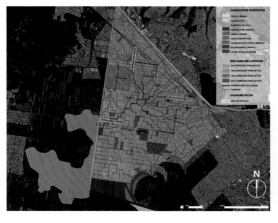

GROUND ECOLOGIES

The Ground Ecologies masterplan proposal for the Jiading District of Shanghai seeks to address the existing 300 x 300 metre (984 x 984 foot) superblocks planned to accommodate a new 500-hectare (1,235-acre) mixed-use development that will potentially host up to 25,000 workers and 200,000 inhabitants. The large blocks of the existing layout produce fragmented urban patches and a homogeneous fabric that fails to generate enough differentiation and a sense of identity within the community. The Ground Ecologies proposal seeks to address this problem in its understanding of the fundamental loss of the human scale within Chinese cities, by reinstating the middle scale. That is, introducing an intermediate urban scale between the domesticity of typical Chinese urban villages and the monumental scale of the superblocks produced by the large-scale highway system. Soil remediation and water treatment systems are used to create an intermediary ground, engendering a series of artificial topographies that knit the site together, and providing diversity through a globally integrated urban system. A map of existing industries is used as an index of potential sources of pollution, which initiates a strategy for the digging and capping of an artificial remedial topography in the form of elongated mounds and ponds oriented towards the prevailing summer winds while blocking those from the north in winter. This topography forms the basis of the spatial proposal, by breaking down the large scale of the primary vehicular system. A series of secondary roads thread through the plan to augment local circulation, and the existing canal system is enhanced as a means of attenuating storm water.

Groundlab, Ground Ecologies, Jiading District, Shanghai, 2010
A newly designed artificial topography is generated through the remediation of polluted soil, creating new infrastructures and new spatial connectivities.

The large blocks of the existing layout produce fragmented urban patches and a homogeneous fabric that fails to generate enough differentiation and a sense of identity within the community.

The ground works and ecological systems proposed for the Jiading masterplan form an organisational strategy for the definition of building typologies.

As part of the ecological remediation of the site, Groundlab's system of excavating and capping polluted soil enhances the environmental and spatial performance of the city.

PRECINT DESIGN
SOIL REMEDIATION TECHNIQUE

THE TECHNIQUES FOR SOIL REMEDIATION VARY ACCORDING TO THE TYPE CONTAMINATION, BUT CONSIST ON REMOVING POLLUTED SOIL (EXCAVATING) OR COVERING IT (CAPPING)

THE COSTS OF REMEDIATING THE SOIL BEFORE IT IS BUILD UPON ARE MUCH LOWER THAN THE COST GENERATED BY THE DIFFICULT STRUCTURAL DESIGN IN THIS TYPE OF SOIL.

SOIL CONTAMINATED BY METAL
金属污染

SOIL CONTAMINATED BY OIL
油污染

SOIL CONTAMINATED BY HEAVY OIL
重油污染

SOIL CONTAMINATED BY METAL
金属污染

SOIL CONTAMINATED BY OIL
油污染

SOIL CONTAMINATED BY HEAVY OIL
重油污染

OVERALL DESIGN 总体设计

SOIL REMEDIATION
土壤整治方案

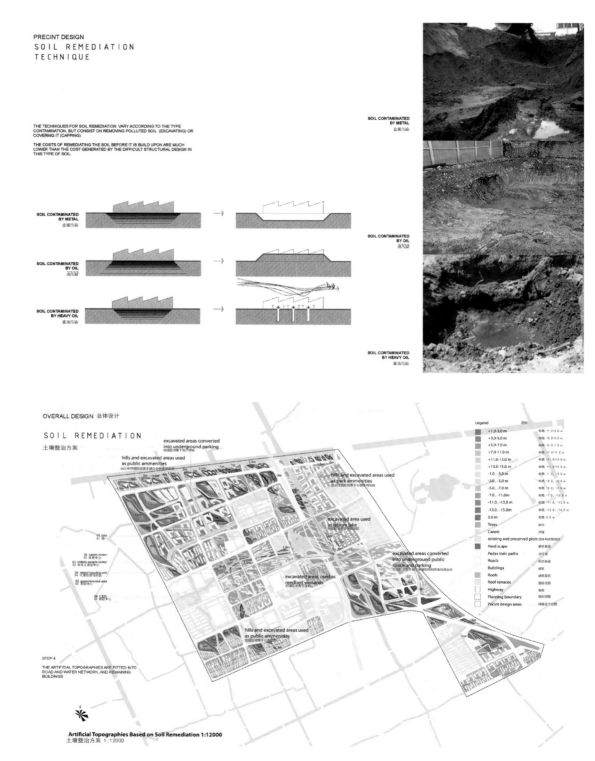

excavated areas converted into underground parking

hills and excavated areas used as public ammenities

hills and excavated areas used as park ammenities

excavated area used as leisure lake

excavated areas converted into underground public space and parking

excavated areas used as reedbed wetlands

hills and excavated areas used as public ammenities

STEP 4
THE ARTIFITIAL TOPOGRAPHIES ARE FITTED INTO ROAD AND WATER NETWORK, AND REMAINING BUILDINGS

Artificial Topographies Based on Soil Remediation 1:12000
土壤整治方案 1:12000

Legend 图例
+1.0-3.0 m
+3.0-5.0 m
+5.0-7.0 m
+7.0-11.0 m
+11.0-13.0 m
+13.0-15.0 m
-1.0 - -3.0 m
-3.0 - -5.0 m
-5.0 - -7.0 m
-7.0 - -11.0 m
-11.0 - -13.0 m
-13.0 - -15.0 m
0.0 m
Trees
Canals
existing and preserved plots
Hard scape
Pedes train paths
Roads
Buildings
Roofs
Roof terraces
Highway
Planning boundary
Pricint design areas

Groundlab's strategy to recover the existing canal system uses natural cleansing systems such as wetlands, and aims to integrate the canals within the public realm of the project.

PRECINT DESIGN
INTEGRATED WATER CLEANSING AND LOOP GENERATION

WATER TREATMENT 水处理
WEATLAND AREA 湿地面积

-2-5 m2 per inhabitant

-Time spent in water: 4 days   净水时间：4天

90.000 habitants × 180.000 m2 of weatland area
9万levels × 180000平方米湿地面积
- Assmount of weatlands proposed: 13   设计湿地数量：13
Area per weatland ≈ aprox 1.4 H
每片湿地面积 ≈ 约1.4公顷

TREATMENT PLANTS 水处理植物

-Reference: Red Hook W.P.C.P New York   参考信息：Red Hook W. P. C.P New York

190.000 people   190000人
60 M.G.D. design capacity   60百万加仑设计容量
1294 H drainage area   1294公顷排水区域

Plant size: 5000 m2   种植尺寸：5000平方米

- On site: 本场地：
526 H drainage area   526 公顷排水区域
90.000 people   90000人

Proposed: Two treatment plants. Aprox 2500 m2

设计提出，两片水净化种植，约2500平方米

Soil remediation proposal

based on the pollution values of exising soil condition, generate artificial typography. The main logic is use vally as construction base, hill and mountains are not builtable since the soil is highly polluted. The main spaces generated by articicial typography are as following:
1 excavated areas used as underground parking
2 hills and excavated areas used as public emmenities
3 excavated areas used as wetland reedbed
4 excavated areas used as public emmenities
5 hills and excavated areas used as park emmenities
6 excavated areas used as recreational lake emmenities
7 excavated areas used as underground space and parking

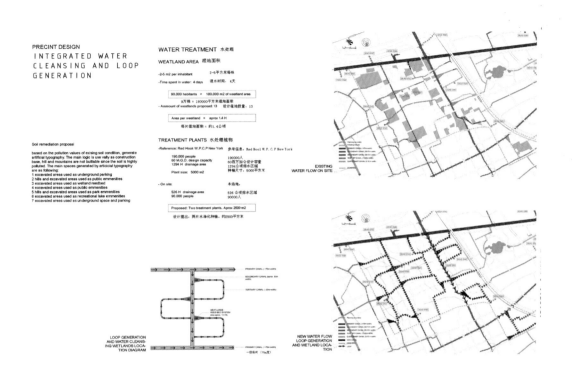

EXGSTING WATER FLOW ON SITE

NEW WATER FLOW LOOP GENERATION AND WETLAND LOCATION

LOOP GENERATION AND WATER CLEANSING WETLANDS LOCATION DIAGRAM

一级河流（75m宽）

OVERALL DESIGN 总体设计
CANAL SYSTEM PROPOSAL
城市特色

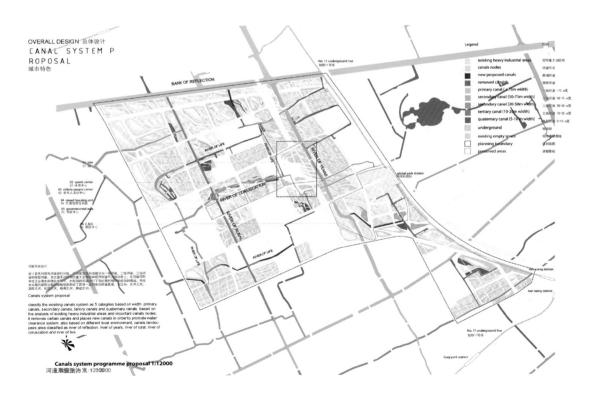

Legend [图例]

existing heavy industrial areas	现状重工业区用地
canals nodes	河道节点
new proposed canals	新增河道
removed canals	拆除河道
primary canal (+75m width)	一级河流 +75 m宽
secondary canal (50-75m width)	二级河流 50-75 m宽
secondary canal (20-50m width)	二级河流 20-50 m宽
tertiary canal (10-20m width)	三级河流 10-20 m宽
quaternary canal (5-10 m width)	四级河流 5-10 m宽
underground	地下河道
existing empty space	现状空地
planning boundary	规划边界
preserved areas	保留用地

河道系统设计

设计先对现存河道进行分级，河道根据宽度分为五级：一级河流、二级河流、三级河流和四级河流，基于对现状重工业区和重要河道节点的分析，在对现有河道中存在工业垃圾的部分填埋，并在别的场地增加新河道，以此来提高河道清理系统。另外，基于当地不同情况河流景观被分级为：映射之河，岁月之河，静谧之河，鼎沸之河和生命之河。

Canals system proposal

classify the existing canals system as 5 catagries based on width: primary canals, secondary canals, teriory canals and quaternary canals. based on the analysis of exising heavy industrial areas and important canals nodes, it removes certain canals and places new canals in order to promote water clearance system. also based on different local environment, canals landscpaes area classifed as river of reflection, river of years, river of rural, river of corrusication and river of live.

Canals system programme proposal 1:12000
河道规划设计方案: 1:12000

In order to define the physical structure of the masterplan, Groundlab's spatial strategy indentifies the earthworks necessary to remediate the soil while at the same time creating an optimum topographical arrangement.

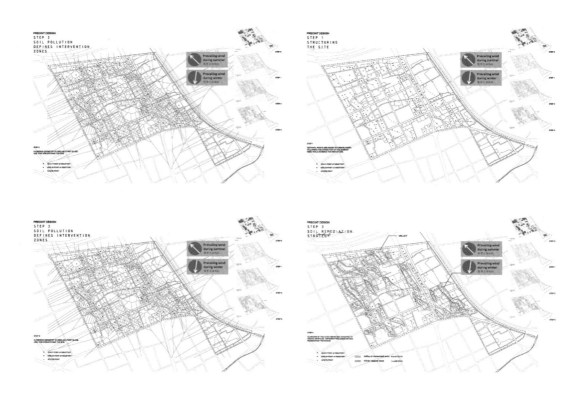

Ground Ecologies proposes the redesign of the existing city superblocks through the remediation of soil and water treatment systems to foster the grounds for a more comprehensive urban development.

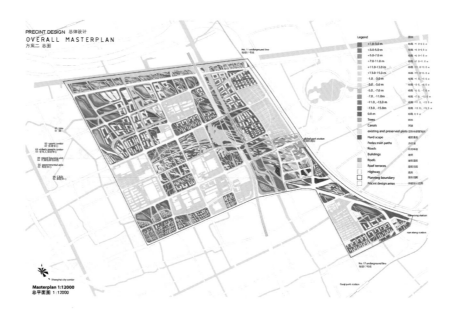

The generation of an artificial topography thus becomes central in the way in which the redesign of the city is thought. Ground Ecologies employs cutting and capping the landscape as an ecological strategy for soil remediation that is capable of producing spatial and urban system effects across numerous scales. In cases where pollutants in the ground may take too long to reduce in toxicity, the most economic option for remediation is to concentrate the polluted land in specific areas and cover it with an impermeable clay or polypropylene membrane. These large pockets of contaminated soil are also an integral part of the network of artificial topographies, isolated from the groundwater to prevent the migration of pollutants, but part of the landscape for public use. Within the same system, small-scale modifications to the ground form the basis of an organisational system that further affects the definition of building typologies. These smaller artificial topographies work as an extended 'plinth' in which buildings are inserted, acting as spatial infrastructure and defining architectural massing according to environmental parameters.

Ground Ecologies deploys a fluid built form that incorporates a new infrastructural sensibility with the aim of producing new open-space morphologies. Here, an activated ground engages with the landscape, road system and water retention ponds, forming a cohesive amalgam that generates a network of uncharted unbanity.

Ground as a New Source of Urbanity

Through a repositioning of the idea of ground, the concept of landscape begins to move from an aesthetic element to one of a performative nature, integrating ecological systems with the infrastructural, and creating new definitions of urban space. Landscape ceases to be an afterthought or a discipline linked to the postproduction of a given masterplan, and is instead a productive mechanism capable of enhancing and generating urban ecological systems, spaces and morphologies. The ground thus no longer exists as a landscape feature, but as an architectural design driver for urban topographical infrastructure. ᐁ

Notes
1. The ground here is understood as a medium materially capable of embodying the qualities that the emergent discipline of landscape urbanism puts forward as design principles.
2. For more on Frederick Law Olmsted, see the National Association for Olmsted Parks: www.olmsted.org.
3. For more on the Emerald Necklace, see http://tclf.org/landscapes/emerald-necklace.
4. For more on the Bronx River Parkway, see http://tclf.org/landscapes/bronx-river-parkway.

Business area typology definition. Ground ecologies define different typologies according to the proposed programmes.

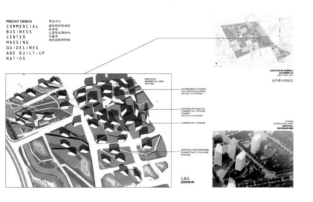

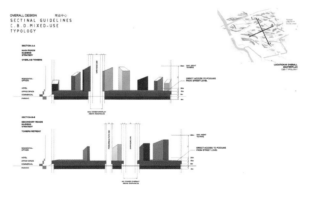

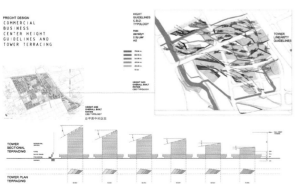

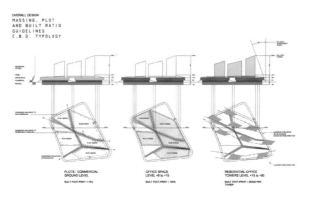

By likening the process of urban design to the diagnostics and intervention of the routine blood test, **Keith Besserud, Mark Sarkisian, Phil Enquist and Craig Hartman** of Skidmore, Owings & Merrill (SOM) provide a powerful biological metaphor for the city and its metabolic flows. Through their descriptions of SOM's work on the Great Lakes Vision (2009), Chicago Lakeside (2012) and the Pin-Fuse Joint (2009), they illustrate the impact of metabolic flows of energy, information and matter at the scale of the regional, urban and architectural.

Keith Besserud, Mark Sarkisian,
Phil Enquist and Craig Hartman

SCALES OF METABOLIC FLOWS

REGIONAL, URBAN AND BUILDING SYSTEMS DESIGN AT SOM

One of the most common medical procedures prescribed by doctors to get a sense of a patient's health is a routine blood test. This is because the blood that circulates through the body is teeming with molecular indicators of health. The bloodstream is like the body's 'postal service', delivering critical molecular signals to all of its physiological systems. At any given moment, billions of chemical molecules are flowing throughout the body, attaching themselves to specific cells and triggering chemical reactions within the cells to keep the body functioning properly. By measuring the chemical content in a patient's bloodstream, anomalies can easily be identified that help the doctor diagnose illnesses and establish how far the patient is deviating from a normal or healthy condition.

This biological process of coordinating interactions between all the physiological systems of the body via the reading, processing and transformation of chemical molecules is what is commonly referred to as 'metabolism'. Metabolic systems are essentially information-processing systems, regulating the flows of biological information and instructions.

Pharmaceutical scientists are also very interested in metabolic processes. The drugs they develop are doses of molecular chemical information that get absorbed into the body, thereby introducing new signals into the body's metabolic flows. Ideally, the drugs are designed to address very specific cells and to communicate very specific instructions. However, because of the enormous biological complexity of our bodies, the great challenge is to accurately predict that the chemicals released will bind only to the specific cells targeted and will introduce only the specific instructions intended. The result of a poor design is side effects. The result of an effective design is a better quality of life.

Within this framework there are two related but discrete modes: diagnosis and intervention. Procedures like blood tests provide important diagnostic indicators of the metabolic status of the body. Intervention, on the other hand, whether it involves medicine, surgery or genetic engineering, is a very different mode, requiring the ability to predict that a certain intervention will achieve the preferred outcome. This second mode is fundamentally a process of design.

BIOLOGICAL ANALOGIES WITH THE URBAN DOMAIN

Going back at least as far as Jane Jacobs, the history of urban theory is replete with analogies between biological systems and metabolic metaphors. Like biological systems, cities and their various urban systems are perpetually 'metabolising' flows of information, energy and matter to drive their processes. People are constantly processing the signals of the city and making decisions based on those signals as they socialise, engage in commerce, interact with the city's infrastructure and consume local natural resources. Information is constantly in motion, enmeshing people, transit systems, retail systems, governance systems, environmental systems, energy systems, educational systems and all the other urban systems into one enormously complex organism.

As with biological systems, we may also consider the metabolic flows of cities through the same two related but distinct lenses of diagnosis and intervention. The diagnostic question of how to measure a city's health is one that is attracting a great deal of global attention. In the absence of predefined standards, cities are crafting their own sets of urban metrics in order to better manage their affairs. Categories of measurement include public safety, public health, education, transportation, jobs, cost of living, local culture and the environment. Specific indicators range from the near universal (for example, commuting times, graduation rates) to the more local (manatee deaths in the city of Jacksonville's local waterways).

The enormous amount of information that feeds into these metrics represents a form of 'big data', which comes from open data movements within governments and NGOs, the physical instrumentation of the city, and the explosion of social media. As a result, new and innovative forms of urban 'blood tests' are quickly emerging to help understand urban metabolic flows. The idea that better metabolic flows, enabled with big data, will lead to better cities underpins the philosophy of the 'smart' cities movement.

SOM, Poly International Plaza, Beijing, due for completion 2015
The multistorey, elliptically shaped diagrid system is designed to support the perimeter of the structure without columns, and to create a double-wall exterior enclosure to control temperature effects on internal spaces.

However, as with the design of drugs, the move from diagnosis to intervention with respect to urban systems is not simple. The great challenge for urban designers and policy makers in dealing with the complexities of urban systems is to intervene with the existing metabolic flows to achieve the intended results without triggering undesirable side effects (for example, lack of affordable housing, ineffective public spaces, unsustainable development). Currently, our abilities to reliably predict the holistic fallout of an urban design or public policy proposal – in terms of social, economic and ecological effects – are limited to relatively simplistic pairings and based primarily on experienced intuition.

SCALES OF FLOWS

The metabolic processing of energy, information and matter happens at a wide range of scales, from the molecular to the cosmic. As urban designers, architects and engineers we are most familiar with the band within this spectrum that ranges from the regional to the urban to the architectural.

The Regional Scale

The story at the regional scale begins with an understanding of how the introduction of humans and human systems impacts the metabolic flows of energy, information and matter within the vast natural ecosystems of the region. In addition to issues such as habitat modification, resource overconsumption and pollution, these problems often become even more complicated at the regional scale because of the introduction of artificial information barriers in the form of jurisdictional geopolitical boundaries.

The Great Lakes watershed in North America provides a very good study of the complexities of the regional scale. The current challenges are related not so much to the human consumption of the water (only about 4.2 per cent of the population's drinking water comes from the Lakes), but rather the systemic treatment of the water and the aquatic ecosystems. The ecosystems are being impacted by multiple factors that cause changes to the molecular constitution of the water of the Lakes, rendering it unable to perform critical metabolic functions and leading to cascading breakdowns of metabolic flows throughout the connected ecosystems.

Harmful farming practices include the use of toxic pesticides, fertilisers that are rich with phosphorous (which accelerates the growth of oxygen-depleting algae blooms that lead to aquatic 'dead' zones), and the lack of erosion control. Logging practices remove shading from streams, altering solar exposures, increasing water temperatures and upsetting spawning patterns. More than 180 non-native species of plants, fish, molluscs and other living things now inhabit the Lakes, altering the aquatic food chain and threatening food supplies and fishing economies. The majority of the industrial energy production plants in the region are coal powered, releasing high levels of carbon dioxide into the atmosphere and depositing toxic mercury into local water sources. Damage from urbanisation includes runoff of untreated storm water, periodic outflows of untreated sewage from combined sewer systems, and the depletion of local water tables. Greatly complicating efforts to coordinate

SOM, King Abdullah City for Atomic and Renewable Energy, Saudi Arabia, 2011
For the conceptualisation studies for a new city in Saudi Arabia, designers wrote a 'raindrop' algorithm that used topographic data to simulate the flow of water into the wadis from different points on the ridges, constrained to different angles of descent. The paths of the water drops served as the starting point for formally organising some of the early design schemes for the project.

remediation strategies is the fact that the watershed region spans the border of two different countries. Stakeholders on the US side include eight different states, 213 counties and 58 Native American reservations. In Canada, there are two provinces and 87 First Nations reserves. Combined, there are over 15,000 cities and towns. All of these jurisdictional borders tend to create impervious barriers to information flows that are critical to the preservation of this vital natural resource. In the absence of this free flow of information to coordinate behaviour, self-preservation instincts will prevail and will only accelerate the deterioration of the Lakes.

In response to this breakdown of trans-jurisdictional information flows, and in the absence of any unifying doctrine, SOM has developed a comprehensive, transnational 100-year vision for the Great Lakes and St Lawrence River region. Conceived as a contribution to the centennial commemoration of Daniel Burnham's 1909 *Plan of Chicago* (which itself was a regionally focused vision that understood Chicago within its greater context), the Great Lakes Vision (2009) presents a message intended to cut through jurisdictional boundaries. Its components address the challenging issues described above, organised into themes relating to urban design best practices, tourism, the enlistment of local research universities, water stewardship advocacy, renewable energy, regional transit systems, moving beyond a carbon-based economy, and local food initiatives. SOM's active promotion of the Vision among countless government and community groups led to its unanimous approval in 2010 by the Great Lakes and St Lawrence Cities Initiative, an organisation representing 73 cities in the US and Canada.

The Urban Scale

At the urban scale, the focus on metabolic flows shifts largely to engineered infrastructure systems built to accommodate the movement of people, energy, water, waste and data across the city. As an example, Chicago Lakeside (2012) is an almost 243-hectare (600-acre) brownfield redevelopment project located on the south end of Chicago where the US Steel South Works steel plant once anchored a vibrant urban neighbourhood. Closed in 1990, dismantled and environmentally remediated, the project site now presents a unique opportunity: the design of a major urban

SOM, Great Lakes Vision, Chicago, Illinois, 2009
top: Agricultural practices represent as significant a threat to the aquatic ecosystems of the Great Lakes as urban pollutants. Increased runoff of sediments and chemicals creates disruptions of natural metabolic processes in the lakes as well as in the soils.

bottom: The network of Great Lakes shipping routes represents the largest freight transport system in North America, delivering iron ore, coal, agricultural grains and other commodities to national and international ports where they are processed into steel, energy, food and many other products.

reinforce the existing commercial corridors by developing extensions that run through the new development.

Movement within the Lakeside community is addressed with strategies to enhance walkability. In order to encourage pedestrian activity, the project incorporates design principles that emphasise small blocks which enable walkable access to a wide mix of essential uses, appropriate levels of density to activate the public spaces, pedestrian comfort through the strategic shading of the sidewalks, and the creation of a network of public green spaces that weave throughout the development, providing contiguous flows across the development not only for humans, but also for local wildlife species.

The management of water at Lakeside represents an attempt to restore natural hydrological balances to the site. The city of Chicago manages storm water in a combined sewer system that mixes the storm water with the sewage from buildings, and then subjects it all to the same energy-intensive purification processes. Furthermore, Chicago draws its

intervention, integrated into a major developed city, on a waterfront site that is essentially a blank canvas.

The urban design is essentially a study of urban systems flows, starting with the flows of people. The masterplan for the transportation/mobility systems builds on the need to accommodate three different types of connections. The first are the connections to downtown Chicago, which is about 18 kilometres (11 miles) to the north. The second are the connections to the adjacent existing communities. The third are the interconnections within the Lakeside development itself. For the connections to Chicago, proposed schemes include the addition of a spur to the existing commuter train line that runs to the west of the site, the introduction of a water taxi service running along the Lake Michigan shoreline, and an extension of Lake Shore Drive, which is a principal vehicular artery running along the eastern edge of the city.

Connections to the adjacent communities are intended to break down perceptions of the Lakeside development as an island, and instead integrate it with the adjacent communities, particularly by creating links to connect the communities to the publicly dedicated lakefront. Proposals here include east–west bike routes that stitch together the communities and the development, and a plan to

SOM, Chicago Lakeside, Chicago, Illinois, 2012
top: Strategies for grafting and assimilating the proposed Lakeside community into its greater urban context include proposals to reinforce three different scales of connectivity: connections to the commercial core of the city; connections to the adjacent communities around the development; and connections within the various districts of the development itself.

SOM, Great Lakes Vision, Chicago, Illinois, 2009
bottom: A coordinated international strategy to protect the Great Lakes remains a work in progress, meaning thousands of individual city and county jurisdictions are obliged to define their own terms of engagement with the Great Lakes basin and its ecological systems.

water from Lake Michigan, but releases its treated sewage into a watershed that flows into the Mississippi River, creating an undesirable open-loop system. For Lakeside, a respect for the natural hydrologic flows is proposed. In the masterplan, both the storm water and the water drawn from the lake ultimately end up in the lake. On-site district-scale treatment facilities are planned, as well as the incorporation of bioremediation strategies for treating the storm water in a more natural, less energy-intensive way. Furthermore, again tapping into the local hydrologic resources, the cold Lake Michigan water that is drawn to support the city's water consumption needs passes through a heat exchange system that would pre-cool the water used for the air conditioning of buildings in the development, creating a reduction in the energy required for building cooling.

The management of the water touches on the final area of focus with respect to flows at the urban scale: the infrastructure systems. Several strategies that develop a high level of synthesis among the energy, water, waste, heating and cooling systems are proposed, and particularly those that leverage heat exchanges in order to reduce energy demands. The information exchanges between the infrastructure systems that are necessary to build these kinds of efficiencies will require appropriate investment in broadband information communication technology (ICT). This ICT investment is also critical to the human component of Lakeside, enabling the people to connect with each other and with the outside world.

The Architectural Scale

Like cities and regions, buildings also metabolise energy, information and matter. Metabolic flows of water, electricity, waste, data, heat, daylight, solar radiation and, of course, people are constantly being processed to keep the building's systems operating effectively. Like a cell within its larger biological context, these flows integrate the building and its systems into the larger urban and natural context.

It may not be readily apparent, but the structural system of a building is actually a good example of a metabolic system. In this case it is energy that is being metabolised – in the form of structural loads and forces. The live and dead loads that are applied to the building are systematically transferred from structural subsystem to subsystem, ultimately finding resolution in the ground. One of the main objectives in designing the structural system is to size the components according to the forces that will be flowing through them; an optimal system is one that allocates the least amount of material and/or cost necessary to accommodate these flows while maintaining a prescribed factor of safety.

Seismic events present a special challenge to the design of a building's structural system because of the largely unpredictable nature of the force trajectories, magnitudes and durations. These types of shocks are fundamentally different from the forces of gravity and wind, and require a special approach to design that deals with the building's stiffness and damping characteristics. By lengthening a building's characteristic period (making it less stiff), the demands on the structural systems from ground motions can be lessened, and the probabilities of minimising damage and returning the building to safe service can be increased.

9% to Chicago's combined sewer

26 acres

595 acres

91% filtered and returned to Lake Michigan

Three common types of active strategies for lengthening the building's period include damping, seismic isolation and dynamic fixity. Damping strategies are used to reduce the amplitudes and resulting accelerations of the building motions, and are an effective way of reducing seismic demand as well as the effects of wind. Seismic isolation is a response strategy that relies on the ability to isolate the building from ground motions.

A third type of seismic response strategy involves dynamic fixity. SOM's Pin-Fuse Joint system is an example of such a system. It behaves with a rigid demeanour much like a conventional moment connection between a beam and a column when subjected to typical wind and gravity loads, or even moderate earthquakes. However, if a dynamic shock is sudden and strong enough, the joint is designed to release and rotate, allowing the connection to slide while dissipating energy through friction heat rather than yield or fracture.

Once the seismic event has passed, the joint is intended to return to its original configuration, using, for example, a sinew-like material such as nickel titanium or some other shape memory alloy. In the future, another type of fixity joint system could incorporate the modulation of clamping forces by introducing heat into the joint fastenings to elongate the bolts.

Implicit in this type of structural system is a feedback loop of flows in which a response is triggered by the detection of induced energy. The detection mechanisms may be localised to the building or may take the form of a sensory field that blankets the entire region and connects to all the buildings within the coverage area. In this scenario, the ability to detect seismic motions at the epicentre could not only provide valuable seconds of advance warning to 'smart' seismic response systems in the building, but could also generate important data about magnitude and motion trajectories. Following the earthquake, additional sensors embedded in the structural

SOM, Digital model of San Francisco, California, 2012
top: SOM's research into the creation of more intelligent urban modelling frameworks includes the incorporation of buildings, infrastructure systems and various dynamic agents that can be attributed with different types of data, integrating across multiple urban systems to reveal insights into urban behaviour and allow for the study of hypothetical urban interventions.

SOM, Pin-Fuse Joint, 2009
above right: The Pin-Fuse Joint (US Patent 6681538) is designed to alter the characteristics of a structure during a strong earthquake by fusing or slipping, dissipating energy through friction, and reducing inertial forces while remaining elastic and allowing for immediate reuse.

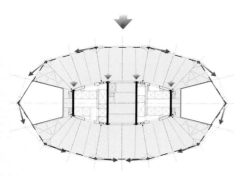

system could be designed to report back on the condition of the structure, making it much easier to understand the building's fitness for safe occupancy. All these flows of energy are examples of structural metabolic processes in which the energy flows become information inputs that lead to physical transformations of materials or mechanisms.

DRAWING FROM BIOLOGY FOR FUTURE POSSIBILITIES

Metropolitan regions, urban districts and even individual buildings all exhibit similarities to biological systems with respect to the ways in which they process (metabolise) energy, matter and information in cascades of feedback loops in order to sustain their vital functions.

In the fields of biology and the medical sciences, revolutionary advances in knowledge have been made in recent decades with respect to understanding the metabolic processes of various natural systems. These leaps in knowledge have been generally preceded by advances in scientific technologies. Brain imaging technologies have transformed the field of neurobiology, enabling doctors and scientists to observe the movements of electrical signals and the sequences of triggers across the neural pathways of the different regions of the brain, and to correlate these movement patterns with other physiological functions. DNA sequencing technologies have allowed biologists and scientists to begin to decode the relationships between strings

of nucleotides and processes of cellular and physiological development. In fact, these advances have fundamentally transformed the field of biology from a focus on flows of energy to one on flows of information.

These recent advances in biology have led to the development of much more sophisticated parametric biological models that can simulate the complexities of interactions between the various physiological systems and agents, and test the efficacies of various proposed treatments in virtual experiments. These virtual experiments, in turn, help build stronger theoretical foundations of biology that drive medical innovation at an ever deeper and faster pace.

As computational technologies continue to work their way into architecture, urban design and related fields of study (for example, sociology, economics, natural ecologies, infrastructure engineering), a similar paradigm is beginning to emerge. Fundamental principles of urban design relating to concepts like density and land use designation that have been incorporated into practice based largely on anecdotal evidence are now poised for a much higher level of scientific insight.

As more sophisticated computational tools begin to emerge we will be able to explore more and more difficult questions such as 'What is the ideal distribution of development density across the city to maximise quality of life?', 'How do design decisions impact the development of social capital in urban neighbourhoods?', and even something so basic as 'What constitutes a neighbourhood?'. As other sciences like sociology and economics continue to develop computational modelling paradigms, the abilities to leverage knowledge embedded in models across discipline boundaries promises to enrich all of those engaged.

Metabolic flows and transactions are at the heart of all of these types of models. Through the use of these technologies we stand to gain a much better understanding of the metabolic patterns of cities, a stronger theoretical foundation regarding the fundamental nature of cities, and a greater ability to intervene. ⚙

SOM, Poly International Plaza, Beijing, due for completion 2015
Force flow diagram through the perimeter structural system consisting of concrete-filled steel pipes. In the future, perimeter systems will be designed to be self-reflective, capable of state changes or interactive material placement through recorded information inputs based on energy flows.

Wolf Mangelsdorf

METASYSTEMS OF URBAN FLOW BURO HAPPOLD'S COLLABORATIONS IN THE GENERATION OF NEW URBAN ECOLOGIES

When regarded as a whole, the flows of a city – made up of people, water, energy, information, materials and waste – constitute a large and complex 'metasystem'. **Wolf Mangelsdorf**, Head of Structural Engineering at Buro Happold, describes a number of projects that Buro Happold has collaborated on with architects, urban planners and landscape architects that mark a significant shift in the design of urban infrastructures, recognising the importance of the metasystems of flow.

Ludwig Hilberseimer, Hochhausstadt, 1924
The concept of utilitarian infrastructure, based on the calculation of transport flows and the separation of spaces and usages, was one of the main concepts that governed the design of the city in the 20th century.

Ecology is the study of the relations of living organisms to each other and to their environment. For ecologists, 'sustainable' biological systems are those, for example forests or wetlands, which persist through time by adaptation at multiple scales to fluctuations and changes in the processes and flows of their environmental context. By contrast, the current emphasis in urban 'sustainability' is all too frequently reduced to energy efficiency and the reduction of emissions. There is, however, a growing trend towards a broader approach in city and infrastructural design projects that is closer to a true ecological concept.

Urban ecology may be considered as a special subset of ecology, one that is focused on the distinct biota and processes that have emerged within urban areas and, more rarely, may also include the study of human cultural systems and their spatial phenomena. In regard to the infrastructure of urban flows, its individual components such as railway stations are embedded in, and inextricably entwined with, all the systems of the city. They contribute to an integrated network of systems that organise the patterns and distribution of flows: primarily of people, but also of water, energy, information, materials and waste. Each of these systems of flow has an effect on the other systems as well as on the urban morphology. When regarded as a whole they constitute a large and complex 'metasystem' that emerges from a collective of subsidiary systems, with many connections and feedback loops between them.

The Efficient City

The design of urban infrastructure has for decades been driven by a notion of technical efficiency determined by simple equations of flow. Number of cars at a given speed determines the width of roads, and pedestrian flows generated by key attractors – stadia or railway stations for instance – result in route layout, width and surface design with little notion of the spatial qualities generated; spaces are separated according to their usage.

Facilitated by increasing car numbers and individual transport, the American city freeway has become the icon of modern urban development. This image of the 20th-century city is now being replicated in the megacities of the Arab world – Dubai is perhaps the best-known example – and applied in the design and planning of 'new cities' in East Asia, particularly the rapidly growing urban centres in China, such as Shanghai, Chongqing or Changsha. This is generating interchangeable masterplans that have their roots in a notion of technically efficient flows, with zoned urban sprawl developing alongside traffic arteries.

There are some fundamental flaws in this approach. The focus on primary measurable flows, which results in a city based on a technical notion of infrastructure, negates any aspect of the informal meta-flows that depend on not being predicted, predictable or designed, but are emergent, allowing for human activity, change and adaptability. As cities are a reflection of our culture, a universal approach to urban development seems an absurd concept. While culture is not static and develops over time, there is a clear understanding that cultural background and development have shaped the spaces and appearance of our cities as well as our urban infrastructure. Moreover, urban ecology and culture are directly linked to climatic conditions. In the past these have been powerful drivers in the development of both city layouts and individual building typologies, creating unique urban or architectural features such as shaded streets, protected squares and courtyards that greatly contribute to the identity of the city they are creating and influence the lives of their inhabitants.

Freeway City
left: American city developments have taken the idea of primary flow systems to the extreme.

Beijing suburb
above: Twentieth-century Western thinking still influences the rapid growth of cities, particularly in the Arab world and in Asia.

Metasystems of Flow

A number of projects in which Buro Happold has collaborated with architects, urban planners and landscape architects mark a shift in the design of urban infrastructure based on recognition of the importance of the metasystems of flow.

Most literally a project of urban ecology is the regeneration (with Moriyama & Teshima Planners) of the Wadi Hanifa in Riyadh. Once a waste dump with virtually no life remaining, this important watercourse in the arid climate of the Saudi capital has been reshaped using a bioremediation facility and natural means to improve the water quality. More significant, however, is that it has been designed as a landscaped park that now attracts visitors as a place of rest, play and social interaction. Early participation of the public in the project and the subsequent adoption by those that use the newly created naturalised parkland will prevent it from returning to being a waste dump again. The ecological aspects of this project, which won the Aga Khan Award for sustainable architecture in 2011, are evident, but the success and transformation of a piece of urban natural landscape lies in the cultural aspects as well as in its climatic qualities.

The High Line in New York City (James Corner Field Operations, Diller Scofidio + Renfro, Piet Oudolf and Buro Happold) works with a similar principle, however rather than transforming a piece of deteriorated natural landscape, it re-appropriates a stretch of 20th-century railway infrastructure. The sequence of urban development here is interesting: originally conceived as a linear park with some extraordinary spatial qualities and a rather unusual perspective on to the city fabric, the High Line alters the pace of movement and becomes an attractor in itself. Over time it has been acting as a catalyst of urban regeneration with a positive impact on the development of the surrounding areas. The definition of the spaces it provides depends primarily on how they are adopted by the users, generating a high level of flexibility and potential for future change reflected in the diversity of developments that have been springing up along its path, including new hotels, street markets, theatres, restaurants and highly sought-after condominiums.

It is this element of future adaptability and lack of definition that increasingly proves to be a means of flow management as well. While the High Line generates an undefined flow alongside being a rather efficient pedestrian connection, exactly the opposite problem occurs in the design of transport infrastructure around key attractors with peak demand, such as stadia. The masterplan for the land around the New Wembley Stadium (Richard Rogers Partnership with Buro Happold) provides a good example of how this thinking became an underlying design principle and at the same time made perfect sense for the developer.

The stadium was initially developed in isolation from the surrounding land characterised by its car park and connection routes to roads, the London Underground and train stations. And pedestrian flow and vehicle traffic stretched the capacity of the supporting rail and road network before and after every event when up to 90,000 people are attracted and released in a very brief period of time. However, in developing the masterplan, this problem was seen as an opportunity. Rather than looking at the impossible task of upgrading the transport system necessary to ease peak flows, the design instead provides the area with enough attractions to entice the spectators to arrive early and remain longer so that the flows can be drawn out over time. This concept finds its analogy in the role of the flood plain in alleviating peak water runoff. An additional benefit of the scheme is the revenue generated by the pubs, restaurants and retail opportunities. As a completely new development that is evolving over time, the biggest challenge here will be to maintain an element of the informal and non-defined as well as the future adaptability required to maintain this.

EARLY PARTICIPATION OF THE PUBLIC IN THE PROJECT AND THE SUBSEQUENT ADOPTION BY THOSE THAT USE THE NEWLY CREATED NATURALISED PARKLAND WILL PREVENT IT FROM RETURNING TO BEING A WASTE DUMP AGAIN.

Richard Rogers Partnership with Buro Happold, Wembley Masterplan, London, 2003–
left: Originally developed by Richard Rogers Partnership with Buro Happold providing all engineering services, the masterplan for the development of the land around the Wembley Stadium addressed the peak flows of the stadium and arena by providing holding spaces, post- and pre-event entertainment and retail. With limited scope for the upgrade of the surrounding transport infrastructure, the delay of arrival and departure alleviates maximum flows. It is planned that the masterplan would be built out over several years by developer Quintain with the possibility for adjustment to maintain the basic concept.

James Corner Field Operations, Diller Scofidio + Renfro, Piet Oudolf and Buro Happold, High Line, New York City, due for completion 2014
below: Key elements of the High Line phases one and two.

bottom right: The third and final phase of the High Line is currently being designed and will complete the loop to the north of the Hudson rail yards.

below top: New York's High Line started as a community concept for the preservation of the derelict elevated industrial railway that runs parallel with 10th Avenue from 14th to 42nd Street. Now entering Phase 3, it is the catalyst for one of the most successful urban regenerations. While the High Line has become a major attraction for locals and tourists, the former industrial areas of the Meatpacking District and Chelsea have been transformed into a prime retail and residential quarter.

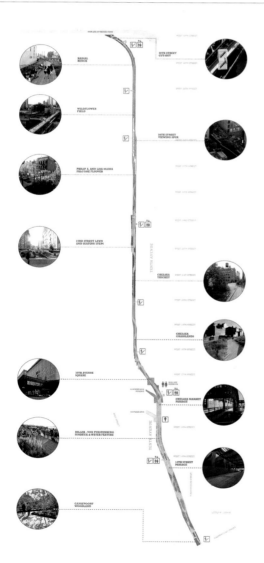

For urban residents, heat islands have many socioeconomic, meteorological and health implications – some positive, some negative, but all influenced by the background regional climate. In humid temperate and hot tropical climates, heat islands can aggravate heat stress and thermal discomfort, especially when building occupants are deprived of a nightly respite from the day's heat load. City dwellers are therefore prone to higher morbidity and mortality rates than rural populations. Air pollution dispersion and external water use in cities are also influenced by the heat island effect, as is the rate of chemical weathering of buildings, monuments and metalwork. Other consequences include higher costs of air conditioning in hot cities, lower frequency of frosts, snowfall and winter road hazards in temperate cities, and more benign conditions for the survival of trees, plants and wildlife in all cities.

The study of urban heat islands has a well-documented history. References to warm cities and cool countrysides first appeared in historical annals of the 17th century, when urban-based thermometer networks detected the artificial warmth of European cities.[6] Hot and polluted atmospheres were then a health concern more than a scientific curiosity, and were hardly investigated for their causes or characteristics. This changed in 1806 when Luke Howard began a monumental study of the climate – including the heat island effect – in London. Howard published his study in 1833 as *The Climate of London*, in which he famously wrote:

> The temperature of the city is not to be considered as that of the climate; it partakes too much of an artificial warmth, induced by its structure, by a crowded population, and the consumption of great quantities of fuel in fires.[7]

The temperature of the city is not to be considered as that of the climate; it partakes too much of an artificial warmth, induced by its structure, by a crowded population, and the consumption of great quantities of fuel in fires.

Howard further observed that certain regions of London with tightly packed buildings and sparse vegetation were warmer, on average, than those of lesser density and with more abundant vegetation. He deduced that such temperature differences must be due to the complex geometry of urban surfaces, the aerodynamic effects of urban roughness, the lack of surface moisture in the city, and the anthropogenic release of heat.[8] These and other discoveries in *The Climate of London* stand today as the foundation of modern science in urban climatology.

In the two centuries that have passed since Howard's groundbreaking work, hundreds of similar but smaller investigations of the urban climate – and especially the heat island – have been reported for cities worldwide.[9] The literature points unequivocally to the conclusion that heat islands are caused mainly by the unique thermal and morphological properties of urban and rural surfaces. Urban climatologists describe and measure these surfaces according to four basic properties of climatological significance: structure, cover, fabric, and metabolism.[10]

Surface structure is the three-dimensional arrangement (that is, the morphology or geometry) of buildings and trees that affects air flow and radiational heating/cooling at the ground. Common measures of structure include street width, building/tree height and sky view factor.[11] Surface cover affects the thermal, radiative and moisture properties of the ground, and is expressed as the fraction of the total plan area occupied by buildings, vegetation and impervious ground surfaces. Fabric is the material composition of natural or constructed surfaces, and in cities it relates to the materials used to construct roads, buildings, parks, gardens and so on. It affects the potential of the surface materials to store and release heat and water. Albedo,[12] permeability, and heat capacity are common measures of the surface fabric. Finally, metabolism is the rate at which a city 'excretes' waste heat, moisture and pollutants from human-based activities such as vehicle combustion, industrial processing and household heating and cooling. Metabolism is also called the anthropogenic heat flux.

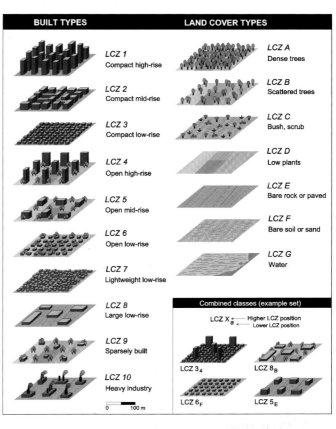

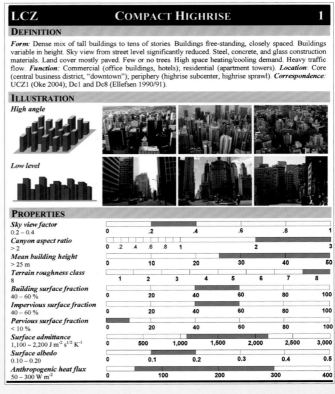

Standard classes of the local climate zone (LCZ) system
top: 'Built' and 'land cover' types can be combined to create new subclasses (see inset).

Sample datasheet for local climate zones
bottom: Datasheets contain LCZ definitions, illustrations and surface properties. The sheets provide useful data to relate city form and function to local climate.

Field measurements in mid-latitude cities confirm that compact morphologies are warmest, followed by open and sparsely built zones, and lastly by treed and low plant zones.

Urban climatologists have recently devised a classification system of the city to relate these measures of the built environment with configurations of city and neighbourhood form at the local scale (that is, hundreds of metres to several kilometres). The new scheme challenges the traditional Western-based notion of cities as separate entities from the countryside, as 'urban' against 'rural.'[13] Such a divisive notion is hardly relevant in a world of 'patchwork', 'polynucleated' and 'borderless' cities, particularly in Asia and the developing world where urban and rural are differentiated not by a boundary or a divide, but by a continuum of land uses, infrastructure and human activities.[14] Urban and rural are also irrelevant in the densely populated corridors that connect these cities, or 'nodes', into vast networks stretching for hundreds of kilometres. A more contemporary classification of the city that is better suited to local climate investigations has evolved from these theoretical perspectives on urban form and urban growth.

In 2004, Professor Tim Oke at the University of British Columbia conceived a new classification of the city to represent local-scale landscapes.[15] The intent behind his classification is to improve siting of meteorological instruments in urban areas, and to standardise communication of urban surface characteristics by climatologists. His scheme of 'urban climate zones' (UCZs) grew from an earlier system of 'urban terrain zones' (UTZs), known more for their architectural detail than climatological merit.[16] The UCZ scheme divides city terrain into seven generalised forms according to their potential to modify the near-surface climate or, in other words, according to surface structure, cover, fabric and metabolism. Users of the scheme can delineate UCZs on a map or aerial photograph of any city, and subsequently deduce a basic understanding of the modified climate.

The UCZ classification has recently been expanded into 'local climate zones'.[17] These consist of 17 classes at the local scale, 10 of which portray urban morphologies that should be recognisable in most cities. LCZs are individually named and ordered by one (or more) distinguishing surface property, which in most cases is the dominant land cover or the height/packing of trees/buildings. 'Compact high-rise' (LCZ 1) is the most intensely built zone, and corresponds to the central core of large modern cities. Its surface is rough (tall, close buildings), impervious (hard, dense cover), dry (little or no moisture or vegetation) and metabolically 'active' (heavy traffic flow, high demand for space heating/cooling). In certain weather conditions, the thermal climate of 'compact high-rise' will differ significantly from that of other zones with contrasting structure, cover, fabric and/or metabolism, such as 'open low-rise' (LCZ 6), 'sparsely built' (LCZ 9) or 'heavy industry' (LCZ 10).

Field measurements in mid-latitude cities confirm that compact morphologies are warmest, followed by open and sparsely built zones, and lastly by treed and low plant zones.[18] Output from computer models of near-surface climate likewise suggests that the diurnal temperature range (the difference between the daily maxima and minima) in each LCZ class decreases significantly with increasing impervious cover and taller and/or more compact buildings.[19] One can easily relate the physical attributes of a local landscape to its observed (or simulated) air temperatures by consulting the standardised datasheets that accompany each LCZ class.[20]

In summary, urban climates and heat islands are closely related to surface cover, building morphology and human activity, and to the flows of energy, mass and momentum that connect the surface and its roughness elements to the enveloping atmosphere. The LCZ system integrates these elements of the surface into standard units of analysis, each embodying the cultural, physical and ecological components of the landscape. This new interpretation of urban space will help researchers to classify cities with greater consistency, objectivity and climatological relevance. It might also help the architects and urbanists who design our cities, and who await reliable and accessible information to link urban form with urban climate. ∆

Notes

1. Timothy R Oke, *Boundary Layer Climates*, Methuen & Co (New York), 1987.
2. The 'surface' is defined as the land-atmosphere interface where climatic processes take place. There are many views regarding where the surface exists. Here it is the complete land-atmosphere interface, meaning the outer 3-D surface area of all objects (for example, building walls and roofs) and the ground (roads, car parks or fields).
3. Helmut E Landsberg, *The Urban Climate*, Academic Press (New York), 1981.
4. Timothy R Oke, 'The Distinction Between Canopy and Boundary-Layer Urban Heat Islands', *Atmosphere* 14, 1976, pp 269–77.
5. See, for example, Kazimierz Klysik and Krzysztof Fortuniak, 'Temporal and Spatial Characteristics of the Urban Heat Island of Lodz, Poland', *Atmospheric Environment* 33, 1999, pp 3885–95, and Timothy R Oke and G Brett Maxwell, 'Urban Heat Island Dynamics in Montreal and Vancouver', *Atmospheric Environment* 9, 1975, pp 191–200.
6. William B Meyer, 'Urban Heat Island and Urban Health: Early American Perspectives', *Professional Geographer* 43, 1991, pp 38–48.
7. Luke Howard, *The Climate of London*, Dalton (London), 1833, p 2.
8. Gerald Mills, 'Luke Howard and *The Climate of London*', *Weather* 63, 2008, pp 153–7.
9. Iain D Stewart, 'A Systematic Review and Scientific Critique of Methodology in Modern Urban Heat Island Literature', *International Journal of Climatology* 31, 2011, pp 200–17.
10. Timothy R Oke, *Initial Guidance to Obtain Representative Meteorological Observations at Urban Sites*, IOM Report 81, World Meteorological Organization (Geneva), 2004.
11. The 'sky view factor' is the percentage of sky hemisphere visible from ground level. It varies with height and density of trees and buildings.
12. 'Albedo' is the ratio of the amount of solar radiation reflected by a surface to the amount received by it. It varies with surface colour, wetness and roughness.
13. George Chu-Sheng Lin, 'Changing Theoretical Perspectives on Urbanization in Asian Developing Countries', *Third World Planning Review* 16, 1994, pp 1–23.
14. Fu-chen Lo and Yue-man Yeung (eds), *Globalization and the World of Large Cities*, United Nations University Press (New York), 1998.
15. Oke, *Initial Guidance*, op cit.
16. Richard Ellefsen, 'Mapping and Measuring Buildings in the Urban Canopy Boundary Layer in Ten US Cities', *Energy and Buildings* 15–16, 1990/91, pp 1025–49.
17. Iain D Stewart and Timothy R Oke, 'Local Climate Zones for Urban Temperature Studies', *Bulletin of the American Meteorological Society* 93, 2012, pp 1879–1900.
18. Iain D Stewart and Timothy R Oke, 'Thermal Differentiation of Local Climate Zones Using Temperature Observations from Urban and Rural Field Sites', *Ninth Symposium on Urban Environment*, Keystone, Colorado, 2010.
19. E Scott Krayenhoff, Iain D Stewart and Timothy R Oke, 'Estimating Thermal Responsiveness of Local-Scale Climate "Zones" with a Numerical Modeling Approach', *TR Oke Symposium & 8th Symposium on Urban Environment*, Phoenix, Arizona, 2009.
20. Iain D Stewart and Tomothy R Oke, 'Local Climate Zones for Urban Temperature Studies', op cit.

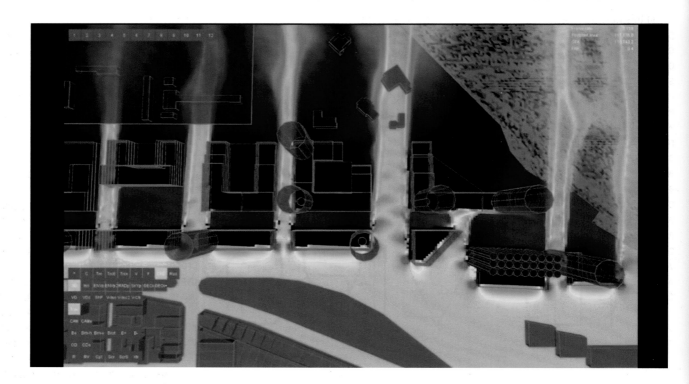

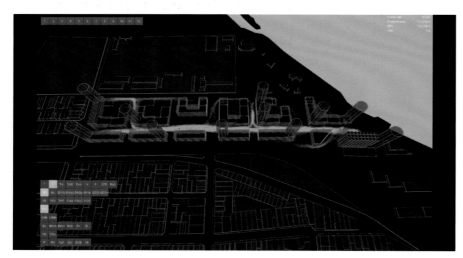

The computer will not replace human experience of the idiosyncrasies that make urban living inspiring. But computational design does provide us with an increasingly sophisticated foil for testing ever-more elaborate hypotheses about what makes cities work.

Foster + Partners, Real-time CFD simulation, 2010–
top: Real-time computational fluid dynamics (CFD) simulation of the prevailing wind behaviour on an urban site. This real-time feedback enables designers to interactively optimise building configuration, to enhance natural ventilation and increase pedestrian comfort.

Foster + Partners, Real-time pedestrian simulation, 2011–
bottom: Real-time pedestrian simulation using an agent approach. Software agents emulate the movement of people on site in terms of wayfinding, and respond in real time to changes in site configuration.

In this way, the energy of the design process can be carried into the real city. Physical considerations, such as daylight, wind and insolation, can be studied at multiple scales and can take into account the complex interactions of existing conditions, as well as changes within a design proposal. New ways of reflecting the experience of a place are also emerging: we are at the beginning of an era in which we can train our design and analysis tools to recognise the most comfortable spots in a neighbourhood, where the combination of shade, sunlight and breeze are just right. We can teach our computers how to recognise an attractive view, or to predict which route pedestrians will prefer as they travel between destinations.

Experience is still the best guide for creating successful cities, especially the understanding gained through the design of previous masterplans such as Masdar City. The computer will not replace human experience of the idiosyncrasies that make urban living inspiring. But computational design does provide us with an increasingly sophisticated foil for testing ever-more elaborate hypotheses about what makes cities work.

Evolution in Silico

Many complex systems demonstrate a paradox where intricate behaviour arises from a set of seemingly simple parts and rules. Every urban environment is composed of a set of interrelated parts, many of which may be uncomplicated when dealt with in isolation, but whose interaction exhibits an array of interesting and emergent trends. Disorganised or organised complexity is prompted by the relationships between these parts, which lay a foundation of multilayered – and often unpredictable – behaviour.

In such complex systems, minimal changes in inputs can have a disproportionate impact on their potential development. In urban environments, the development of a place is impacted by numerous factors whose patterns of interaction are hard to predict, making the potential outcome uncertain at best. The key challenge for designers is to determine how simple changes of the key aspects will propagate throughout the system, and the final effect these changes may have.

These challenges can be addressed by computational platforms that allow for the evolution of systems via simulation processes. Through this *evolution in silico* one can observe the effects that certain changes of initial variables may have, how these propagate through the system, and what the potential responses may be.

Population Thinking

Manuel DeLanda champions the notion of 'population thinking', considering design options as a family, sharing genes of expressed parameterised variation.[2] Those designs which will fare best are more likely to survive an evolutionary design process, and those which do not excel are likely to recede in their influence. Foster + Partners considers population not just in terms of designed populations (buildings, open space designs, regional connections), but also in regard to the numerous inhabitants who will test a design. In this context, the fitness of a design is not at all a simple (linear) function, but instead is a response to a complex, agent-based notion of urban inhabitance.[3]

Agent-based simulation of pedestrian or crowd movement is one such application of this approach. Here, the aggregate behaviours of populations of individuals can be studied following simple rules. Effectively, at every step in a grid of urban open space, an individual moves in the direction that affords them the broadest uninterrupted field of view. Combining this with simple avoidance rules, an evaluation of urban occupation can be obtained which, while crude, still mirrors accepted measures of spatial connectivity. This analysis is sufficiently computationally streamlined that these populations can adapt to design changes – for instance, the change in a building outline – in real time. This allows for the possibility of deploying these agent populations in a genetic simulation of building design ('co-evolution') or of allowing the designer to engage with analysis in an intuitive fashion ('user-defined fitness').

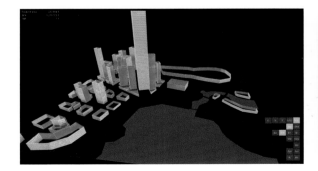

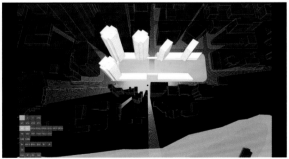

Foster + Partners, Real-time isovist simulation, 2011–
Isovists represent the visible boundary for a pedestrian walking through an urban environment. They provide a feel for the perceived field and depth of view, which can shape the experience of a space and wayfinding within it.

Foster + Partners, Solar simulation, 2010–
Solar analysis tools provide fast feedback on overshadowing, solar gain and daylight.

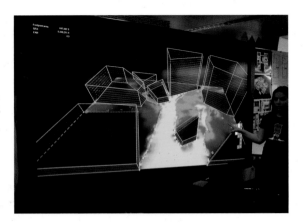

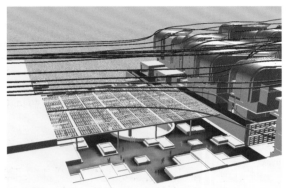

Solely technical approaches to urban design risk delivering sterile urban spaces, in the same way that solely intuitive approaches risk delivering impractical ones.

Foster + Partners, Masdar Institute, Abu Dhabi, 2007–
right: The Masdar Institute is the first phase of Masdar City to be completed, and is a research-driven university with a focus on advanced energy and sustainable technologies.

above bottom: Early real-time immersive walkthrough of the Masdar City project. The additional visualisation of airflow and solar gain allowed designers to better understand the interaction between spatial experience and environmental performance.

Foster + Partners, Interactive masterplanning system, 2010–
top: Interactive masterplanning system. This touch-enabled real-time modelling and simulation system enables architects, urban designers and engineers to engage in a collaborative integrated design process.

Quality Over Quantity

By allowing designers to actively and intuitively engage with analysis, this approach has the potential to bring about a change in the way that analysis data is understood and applied within the design process. Like its counterpart in structural engineering, environmental design and engineering often relies on rules of thumb in the early stages of design. This is rightfully so, as designers with a sensitivity for comfortable, enjoyable places can often anticipate the feeling of a prospective design. It is possible, however, to engage our computational tools to identify some of the same patterns that seasoned designers would recognise, and to do so at a microclimatic scale that would be tedious and exhausting for a designer to do thoroughly.

Continuing the example above, we began to ask how agents might occupy space in a more complex context, taking into account environmental comfort in addition to the intervisibility measures mentioned previously. As a custom-built, bespoke platform is being used for modelling and analysis, it was straightforward to incorporate modules that we had already written to determine sunlight hours, insolation and wind speed at the street level.

This brings yet another level of immediacy to the evaluation of designs such that we can begin to assess how people would move – and where they might congregate – based on the complex patterns of others moving around them, as well as the qualities of light, heat and breeze in their environment.

The analyses discussed thus far attempt to apply quantitative thresholds to notions of how people will behave in the aggregate. For instance, most people in selecting a rest spot while walking across town will avoid overcrowded spaces, and will try to find an optimal microclimate using cues of shadow, awareness of breeze, and other related factors. Such common behaviour can, to an extent, be understood as qualitative, and we are therefore also conducting research into simulations of the urban environment that might be considered more qualitative than quantitative; for example, engaging with the issue of 'quality of view' as an attempt to understand some of the factors in how people conceptualise the aesthetic and informational qualities of urban environments. Using the tools of artificial intelligence, we can intuit how designers or developers might appreciate views – of a prominent landmark, for instance – and then apply this understanding on a scale that would be daunting to undertake without computer automation.

The Creation of Places

Solely technical approaches to urban design risk delivering sterile urban spaces, in the same way that solely intuitive approaches risk delivering impractical ones. Innovative tools and interfaces allow a systematic approach to the place design problem, by incorporating both computation and intuition. Custom applications with radically diminished running times allow designers to investigate a plethora of competing options, and judge – in real time – how these configurations are performing relative to environmental, socioeconomical and aesthetic criteria. Furthermore, the qualitative nature of the outputs enhances the way designers perceive 'cause and effect' in alterations of building topology and morphology, as the impact of each change is directly visible. These tools and processes allow us to take a holistic, integrated approach, where architects, urban designers and engineers can combine the best of human intuition and cultural experience with computational rigour to create true places rather than just spaces. ᗐ

Notes
1. See Peter Katz, Vincent Joseph Scully and Todd W Bressi, *The New Urbanism: Toward an Architecture of Community*, McGraw-Hill (New York), 1994, and Christopher Alexander, *A Pattern Language: Towns, Buildings, Construction*, Oxford University Press (New York), 1977.
2. Manuel DeLanda, 'DeLeuze and the Use of the Genetic Algorithm in Architecture', in Neil Leach (ed), *Designing for a Digital World*, John Wiley & Sons (Chichester), 2002.
3. Neil Leach, 'The Limits of Urban Simulation: An Interview with Manuel DeLanda', ᗐ *Digital Cities*, July/August (no 4), 2009, pp 50–5.

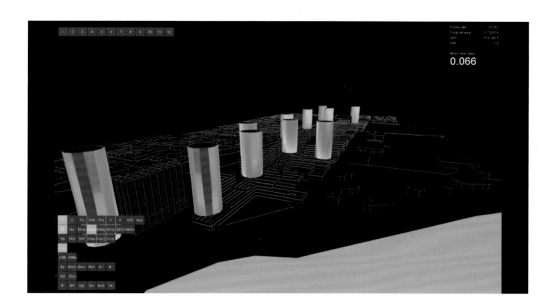

Foster + Partners, View Analysis, 2005–
View analysis, providing quantitative and qualitative measures of views from the building facades.

NETWORKS AND THE CITY

'Cities need to change to survive. As living beings that are constantly replacing their cells, rebuilding their veins and arteries, and pumping energy and matter or producing waste, cities are also growing and evolving as they age.' Just how complex, though, are cities? **Sergi Valverde and Ricard V Solé** of the the ICREA-Complex Systems Lab at the Universitat Pompeu Fabra in Barcelona look at how network theory and emergent dynamics might be bringing us closer to an overarching theory of urban organisation.

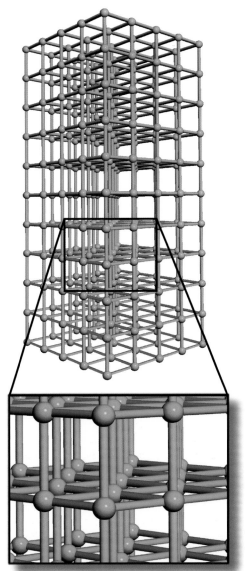

Sergi Valverde, Skeleton frame of a virtual skyscraper, ICREA-Complex Systems Lab, Universitat Pompeu Fabra, Barcelona, 2013
The skeleton of a building forms a uniform grid of horizontal layers. This highly regular organisation is the fingerprint of design and conscious planning.

In Italo Calvino's book *Invisible Cities* (1972)[1] the young Marco Polo describes to the ageing emperor Kublai Khan his recollections about imaginary lost towns. The cities described by the imagined Venetian are themselves the products of imagination, equally poetic and surreal. But in many cases the descriptions capture the essence of what cities are or what they should be. The city of Zora, for example, is said to have something special in the patterns emerging from its streets, doors and windows, sharply remembered by the traveller 'as in a musical score'.[2] However, in order to be easily remembered, the city needed to remain 'motionless and always the same'.[3] As a consequence, 'Zora languished, disintegrated, disappeared. The earth has forgotten her.'[4]

Real cities display complex patterns, which our mind organises and identifies not because of some special set of features, but according to the underlying relationships among buildings, streets and the mark left by time on every object. Indeed, cities need to change to survive. As living beings that are constantly replacing their cells, rebuilding their veins and arteries, and pumping energy and matter or producing waste, cities are also growing and evolving as they age. They need to constantly adapt. Perhaps as it is told in another famous book, Lewis Carroll's *Through the Looking-Glass* (1871), where Alice and the Red Queen run and run as fast as possible, every city needs to constantly change in order to remain in the game. As the Red Queen said to Alice: 'Now, here, you see, it takes all the running you can do, to keep in the same place.'[5]

Cities are at the forefront of our changing civilisation; they will largely shape our future and play a key role in the challenges yet to be faced. And yet we are far from understanding them. As happens with other complex systems, a large number of metaphors have been used in the past to capture their tangled nature and our role in their development, growth and – sometimes – decay. The city has been cast as a steam engine, as an organism or communication network. It is interesting to notice that similar analogies have been used for the brain, probably the greatest challenge for both scientists and philosophers. How complex is a city? A satisfactory answer to this question requires an appropriate view of complexity beyond qualitative metaphors. In the last 20 years, researchers from physics and complex systems sciences have introduced powerful techniques of data analysis that are changing our perspective of cities and suggest that a theory of city organisation might not be far from our reach.[6] Among the weaponry recruited for this goal, network theory appears as an essential component.[7] Networks pervade complexity, and the development of a theory of their origins and meaning (both in natural and man-made systems) has paved our way towards the dream of an overarching urban theory.

Networks are everywhere. Streets define more or less ordered grids enabling the flow of people and vehicles.[8] And buildings are themselves reticulated networks embedded in space and themselves filled by other networks providing the matter, energy and information needed to sustain our lives. There are also some remarkable similarities between city processing mechanisms and biological metabolism. One case study is that of the collective behaviour and nest construction of social insects.[9]

Termites are particularly revealing as examples of emergent dynamics. Individuals are blind and receive information from nearest nest mates. They do not possess a global picture of the nest structure, and yet they are able to build it. The result is a structure that at a termite's scale is colossal (termite mounds can reach heights of several metres),

Collective building behaviour
Social insects like termites form very large colonies composed of many individuals that display collective behaviour, for example building complex nest structures.

and within which the colony sustains itself and provides a stable, safe environment by means of extensive cooperation and parallel information processing.

What kind of structure describes a termite nest? The skeleton of a virtual nest, which has been simulated and compared to real data from 3-D computer tomography techniques after replacing their chambers and the corridors connecting them by nodes (balls) and edges (links), can be visualised in a simplified graph representation.[10] Chambers are used within a colony to store food, take care of eggs and larvae or simply provide shelter. Corridors are excavated by termites as the nest is built to link the different parts of the whole structure. The network of corridors and chambers heats or cools the mound,[11] maintaining a nearly constant internal temperature of 30°C (86°F). Not surprisingly, termite mounds have inspired designs for efficient climate control in buildings.

A closer examination reveals that the internal web of connections is like a distorted lattice that has been created in some disorganised way. This can be seen as a spatial lattice made up by randomly connecting chambers in such a way that the 3-D distribution of them is optimal: a minimal number of corridors has been used that guarantees that the termite colony exploits the greatest amount of space at the lowest cost of expended energy.[12] In this way, the colony of 'blind architects' spontaneously generates a building that, despite its apparent disorder, hides a high degree of structural order. Although not fully obvious from visual inspection, quantitative measures allow the detection of the presence of a noisy lattice: a hidden order has been created out of individual disorder. Though no conscious plans or maps exist, the structure's blueprint is captured internally by the nature of the interactions between individuals. The web of social exchanges defines, to a large extent, the organisational plan, but something else is needed.

Like other man-made artefacts, buildings are the result of purposeful design; however biological structures are not,[13] as their lack of top-down planning requires alternative forms of construction based on bottom-up rules. Such rules very often follow what the French biologist François Jacob named 'tinkering':[14] the massive tendency to reuse made by biological evolution which – as pointed out by Richard Dawkins – operates as a blind watchmaker,[15] unable to foresee the future. When termites build their nests, there is a complex process of interaction between the growing structure and individual behaviour. This interaction between the agents

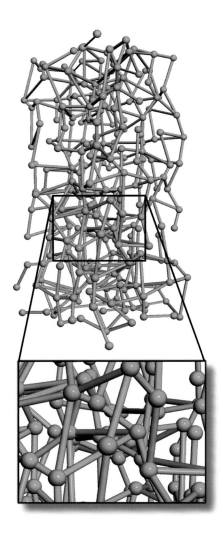

Sergi Valverde, Structure of gallery networks in a termite nest, ICREA-Complex Systems Lab, Universitat Pompeu Fabra, Barcelona, 2013
Virtual cast of a termite nest using 3-D computer tomography. The picture was obtained from volumetric data providing sectional images of a real nest. The 3-D galleries and chambers within the nest were reconstructed from these sections. The structures were then further simplified into a network model, which can be directly visualised in a computer and also enables quantitative measurements of the nest structure.

and the inert, changing structure they are building is called 'stigmergy',[16] and defines an additional noticeable difference between collective intelligence and its artificial counterpart. As the structure grows and changes, so does the way the individuals behave. The structure influences the way the rules evolve so that individual behaviour and structure somewhat change each other. This pattern is also present in biological development, where gene networks responsible for pattern formation are affected by their spatial locations through gradients and boundaries. However, there are limitations to what is actually possible, and this makes biology and technology closer than might be expected. Physics and even mathematical limitations play a leading role here, which can be better appreciated on a larger scale.

Webs within Webs: Convergence

Buildings appear to be one easily identifiable component within a nested hierarchy of webs. They are embedded within local street maps that are part of the global pattern defining the city distribution. Cities are not disconnected elements either: they are connected through several types of transportation networks. The hierarchy ends up in the global web that defines the limitless boundaries of our civilisation.

The realisation that a nested set of webs is at work is important for many reasons. On the one hand, different levels allow us to formulate different questions: typically, what happens at one scale cannot be reduced to the properties of low-level structures. Looking at individual termites does not tell us anything about nest building in the same way that single buildings tell us nothing about city growth. On the other hand, a complete theory of city dynamics should be able to explain multiple levels of organisation, which may require abandoning some well-established assumptions.

An example of the decoupling between levels is provided by the observation that the boundaries of cities often grow in disorganised ways characterised by the same rules that seem to operate for growing tissues. Using Berlin or London as case studies, physicists studying the time evolution of urban boundaries discovered that they expand in ways similar to those of cell cultures or bacteria in Petri dishes.[17] In this case, a very simple model lacking any kind of central control was able to explain the growth of large cities by considering them as living populations expanding to their nearest locations. Denser clusters of local populations would be more likely to occupy nearest, empty spots around them. The global result was a pattern of growth not dissimilar to the rugged boundaries of a growing tumour.

Many natural and artificial networks share common features because they operate under similar constraints including spatial embedding, optimisation and self-organisation. Cities, ant nests and leaf veins are all examples of systems embedded within efficient transportation networks. They are spatial networks whose nodes and links are embedded in space, limiting the density of connections per unit of area. Spatial inhomogeneities, natural barriers and environmental templates also influence their organisation. As a consequence, the physics of pattern formation in these disparate systems leads to common solutions that we perceive as observable regularities. When looking at street maps, we can appreciate a whole spectrum of possible designs: from trees and grids to the more disordered (or organic) patterns. Interestingly, some of these patterns are shared by the galleries excavated by ants.[18] Transportation systems optimised for efficiency and cost are treelike, in that they have no loops. However, observation of leaf veins reveals that many closed loops are required to protect against external damages and fluctuations in load.

London city network
This night aerial view from Bank onto the City of London enables us to compare the flow of urban traffic with the flow of ants within their nests. Cities and nests have comparable scales: millions of individuals live in the city and in the nest. The large scale of these systems requires a transportation network that enables an efficient flow of goods and individuals.

Organic city slums
Aerial view of the Vidigal favela, a slum on the hills behind Copacabana in
Rio de Janeiro. All cities have their slums and informal settlements, often
on the edges of built-up areas. In the 18th and 19th centuries, the term
'rookery' was given to a city slum of poor people due to the perceived
similarities between their disordered layout and the large, noisy colonies
of multiple nests made by rooks. On the other hand, slums appear to be
an inevitable component of dynamic and rapidly changing cities.

Design Through Self-Organisation

Although the tangled organisation of city streets seems too complex in organisation to fit into a simple model, simple computational models can reproduce phenomena that involve the most complex agents such as humans. Physicists Mark Barthélemy and Alessandro Flammini presented a very simple computational model that takes into account spatial embedding and local optimisation rules to generate synthetic (but realistic) urban systems.[20] Several versions of the model exist, and one of the most successful incorporates the interactions between population density and road formation. In broad terms, a road segment is formed, then grows and expands to connect different local 'centres', or neighbourhoods, by linking them in the most efficient way and therefore reducing costs. There is no complex planning, yet very good agreement between the real and the virtual city. The model captures several independent features of real street networks as well as the spatial and temporal organisation of the populations around them – a big achievement for the blind architect.

Is nature telling us something useful about human designs and potential alternative ways of thinking about them? Can future urban planning benefit from exploiting self-organisation in an effective manner? At the largest scale, self-organisation might inevitably occur beyond our control unless large-scale plans are at work before the system starts to grow (a rather unlikely scenario). Allowing self-organisation to be part of the design principles can bring unsuspected novelties, but also undesirable outcomes. It can be a source of spontaneous order, but it has also been recognised as the origin of large fluctuations that eventually result in

Is this similar in cities? Many large cities were, at their origin, a collection of small, disconnected towns. Population flows expanded towns' borders towards nearby local centres, eventually merging them within a larger urban system. What were once empty landscapes of isolated urban centres are now crossed by spatial networks that enable traffic flows and social exchanges. Street planning can be regarded as an optimisation problem that can be expressed as 'for a given number of centres find the transportation network that connects them, and ensure that the density of connections is sufficient to ensure that a path to navigate from one location to another in the network can always be found'.

A modest increase in link density might enable a sudden transition from a disconnected system to a so-called 'percolating network', and this encapsulates an enormous number of important phenomena known to occur in complex systems. It defines the boundary between a set of disconnected objects and a true system where any part is connected to any other through some path. As in leaf veins, further increases in the density of links yield loops and many alternative paths connecting any pair of endpoints, and this in turn leads to safer traffic and a rational distribution of space.[19] The resulting street network is what we easily identify with the city's skeleton, and its statistical organisation (once again) shares many features in common with leaf veins. What is the consequence of this convergent design?

In broad terms, a road segment is formed, then grows and expands to connect different local 'centres', or neighbourhoods, by linking them in the most efficient way and therefore reducing costs.

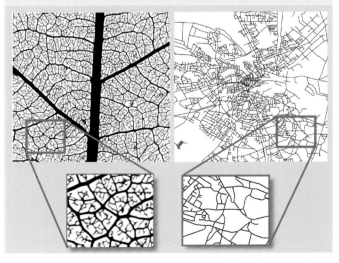

Transportation networks
A comparison of natural and artificial transportation networks reveals common principles of organisation. Leaf veins have many closed loops in order to be robust to exogenous perturbations, like damage and load fluctuations. Likewise, increased density of streets may lead to a rational distribution of traffic loads and efficient transportation systems.

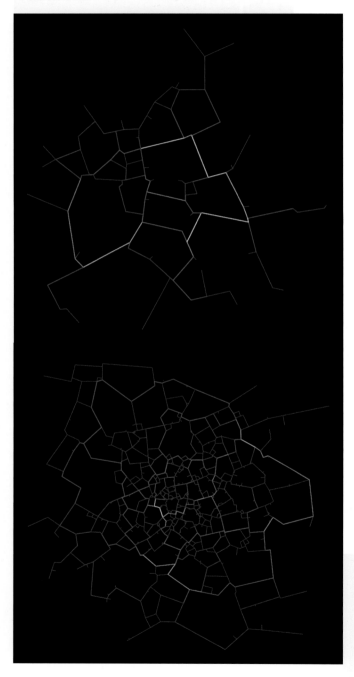

catastrophe. So before we consider using it, we need (as scientists do) to start to understand it.

It is not possible to even imagine what kind of social engineering experiment could modify the large-scale evolution of urban structures. However, at some smaller scales some useful lessons can be extracted. Consider, for example, flows. Networks of flows propagate across the city. Some involve energy and matter while others carry information. And one very special type of agent involves all of them: humans. Due to their obvious relevance and the vast amounts of data that can be acquired about them, pedestrians have been the subject of intense scientific analysis. Walking humans in different scenarios define a particularly interesting problem, and understanding the nature of their collective motion has become a large area of study, for example, for physicists including Dirk Helbing and co-workers.

Helbing and colleagues showed that – against our intuitions – human crowds behave statistically in a rather particle-like fashion.[21] We might think that since these complex agents are intelligent beings, there is no simple model that describes, for example, the spontaneous formation of trails in parks and gardens. Pedestrians prefer to walk frequently used paths: the increased visibility with a large number of footprints results in a reinforcement process and the emergence of a stable trail system. Interestingly, the emergence of trails is very robust and largely independent of specific details of pedestrian behaviour, and they reappear despite the subsequent efforts of urban planners to restore original areas. The lesson? Here crowds act as 'blind designers', and do so against previous (rational) plans and through collective behavioural patterns.

Lessons from *Physarum*

Top-down planning is limited because of the intrinsic difficulties associated with making accurate predictions of the future evolution and growth of cities. But the similarities between natural and artificial networks suggest that we can perhaps learn how to reuse biological solutions. Recent experiments with the slime mould *Physarum Polycephalum* illustrate one remarkable possibility.[22] Here researchers used this single-cell organism to uncover optimal forms of

Walking humans in different scenarios define a particularly interesting problem, and understanding the nature of their collective motion has become a large area of study.

connecting nodes in a graph using efficient transportation paths. Imagine, for example, a set of cities located on a map. We want to design a low-cost, efficient transportation network connecting these locations. As the number of cities grows, so rapidly does the potential number of solutions. The problem becomes a nightmare and no systematic approach can be used to test every solution. However, our organism solves it.

A piece of food is placed in each city location, and the fungus allowed to search through space. Each time it detects a 'city' it grows there, at the same time creating hollow tubes transporting food between neighbouring cities. The tubes are created and destroyed as the living web explores its surrounding space, and the dynamics are dominated by a spontaneous minimisation of the transport system. The final result is a quite well-designed structure that has been shown to give a design solution that is often better than human-designed networks. The potential and elegance of this method allow its application in a disparate range of spatial systems requiring cost minimisation while maintaining a fluid communication. It has yet to be generalised in domains beyond road maps, but its efficiency in quite different case studies is already established and could be a source of novel approaches to network design at different scales. This single-cell living web not only defines optimal paths connecting a complex array of locations, but can also find its way out of the labyrinth. The blind designer might therefore teach us some valuable lessons as to how to escape from our own design traps. ∆

Notes
1. See the English translation from the original published in 1972 in Italian: I Calvino, *Invisible Cities*, Harcourt Brace & Company (San Diego, CA), 1978.
2. Ibid, p 15.
3. Ibid, p 16.
4. Ibid.
5. L Carroll, *Through the Looking Glass*, Macmillan (London), 1897, p 177.
6. See, for example, M Batty, 'The Size, Scale and Shape of Cities', *Science* 319, 2009, pp 769–71; M Batty, 'Building a Science of Cities', *Cities* 29, 2011, pp S9–16; L Bettencourt, J Lobo, D Helbing, C Kühnert and G West, 'Growth, Innovation, Scaling, and the Pace of Life in Cities', *Proceedings of the National Academy of Sciences* 104, 2007, pp 7301–6; and H Samaniego and ME Moses, 'Cities as Organisms: Allometric Scaling of Urban Road Networks, *Journal of Transport and Land Use* 1, 2008, pp 21–39.
7. See M Buchanan, *Nexus: Small Worlds and the Groundbreaking Science of Networks*, Norton & Co (New York). 2003, and MEJ Newman, *Networks: An introduction*, Oxford University Press (New York), 2010.
8. J Buhl, J Gautrais, N Reeves, RV Solé, S Valverde, P Kuntz and G Theraulaz, 'Topological Patterns in Street Networks of Self-Organized Urban Settlements', *European Physical Journal B* 49, 2006, pp 513–22.
9. G Theraulaz, E Bonabeau and J-L Deneubourg, 'The Origin of Nest Complexity in Social Insects', *Complexity* 3, 1998, pp 15–25.
10. A Perna, C Jost, E Couturier, S Valverde, S Douady and G Theraulaz, 'The Structure of Gallery Networks in the Nests of Termite Cubitermes spp. revealed by X-ray Tomography', *Naturwissenschaften* 95, 2008, pp 877–84.
11. JS Turner, *The Tinkerer's Accomplice: How Design Emerges from Life Itself*, Harvard University Press (London) 2007.
12. S Valverde, B Corominas-Murta, A Perma, P Kuntz, G Theraulaz and RV Solé, 'Percolation in Insect Nest Networks:

Evidence for Optimal Design, *Physical Review E* 79, 2009, p 066106.
13. RV Solé, R Ferrer, JM Montoya and S Valverde, 'Selection, Tinkering and Emergence in Complex Networks', *Complexity* 8, 2003, pp 20–33.
14. F Jacob, 'Evolution and Tinkering', *Science* 196 (4295), 1977, pp 1161–6.
15. R Dawkins, *The Blind Watchmaker*, Norton & Company (New York), 1986.
16. E Bonabeau and G Theraulaz, 'A Brief History of Stigmergy', *Artificial Life* 5, 1999, pp 97–116.
17. HA Makse, S Havlin and HE Stanley, 'Modelling Urban Growth Patterns', *Nature* 377, 1995, pp 608–12, and M Batty, *Cities and Complexity*, MIT Press (Cambridge, MA), 2005.
18. J Buhl, J Gautrais, N Reeves, RV Solé and S Valverde, 'Efficiency and Robustness in Ant Networks of Galleries', *European Physical Journal B* 42, 2004, pp 123–9.
19. E Katifori, GJ Szollosi and M Magnasco, 'Damage and Fluctuations Induce Loops in Optimal Transport Networks', *Physical Review Letters* 104, 2010, p 048704.
20. M Barthélemy and A Flammini, 'Modeling Urban Street Patterns', *Physical Review Letters* 100, 2008, p 138702.
21. D Helbing and P Molnár, 'Social Force Model for Pedestrian Dynamics', *Physical Review E* 51, 1995, pp 4282–6, and D Helbing, J Keltsch and P Molnár, 'Modelling the Evolution of Human Trail Systems', *Nature* 388, 1997, pp 47–50.
22. A Tero, S Takagi, T Saigusa, K Ito, DP Bebber, MD Fricker, K Yumiki, R Kobayashi and T Nakagaki, 'Rules for Biologically Inspired Adaptive Network Design', *Science* 327, 2010, pp 439–42.

Self-organised human trails
A spontaneously created path between two roads close to the Barceloneta beach in Barcelona. Pedestrians eschewed the established walkways (the diagonal red-brick path and the horizontal path at the bottom) and created their own paths. Once created, other pedestrians subsequently reinforce the most attractive trails as they reduce physical and navigational costs.

Daniel Segraves

DATA CITY

Daniel Segraves, Urban Energy Data Model, Chicago Loop, 2011
above: A working model of the city and its vast solution space, used to process its energy and flows, requires an equally vast array of data, as evident by the cloud of data shown here.

opposite top: The overall carbon impact attributed to each building relative to its size, shown here in red to represent heavier impact, was calculated using historic and predicted energy use, as well as many externalities such as the flow of goods and people to and from each building.

URBAN METABOLIC DECISION PROCESSES

Designer and computational specialist **Daniel Segraves** describes the decarbonisation tool that he has helped develop in collaboration with Chicago-based Adrian Smith + Gordon Gill Architects and the Argonne National Laboratory Computation Department. The creation of the multi-scale analytic model focusing on the embodied and expended carbon of urban systems allows for energy performance to be tracked across a wider region, encompassing multiple buildings and agents.

Cities are in constant evolution, developing the ability to perceive and process vast amounts of information. This sentience is guided by a series of decision-making processes capable of managing the growth and transformation of the city. These decision processes, proposed here as analytical models, must access immense arrays of data and traverse large solution spaces. This data must be historic and live, morphological and technological, of flows and of material – energy, water, waste, people, goods, air and structures. The processes thus become a working model of the city, as well as every possible manifestation of it – both present and future.

The work discussed here is an ongoing, collaborative development of a multi-scale analytic model as a critical aspect of the decarbonisation of urban environments, built on research and development undertaken by Chicago-based Adrian Smith + Gordon Gill Architecture with the Argonne National Laboratory Computation Department. It is intended to function as a design, planning and communication tool focused on the embodied and expended carbon of urban systems, both present and predicted. As opposed to the traditional approach for energy performance contracting that addresses buildings as discrete elements and building owners independently, this model allows for energy performance contracting to be expanded to a larger region encompassing multiple buildings and agents.

Model Function

The tool is applied to a network of buildings in geographic proximity, as well as to a distributed network of buildings, leveraging morphological and dynamic data arrays. The primary function is an optimisation module programmed to determine the most efficient allocation of a given amount of resource towards growth or reconfiguration of the agents in question. With a specified amount of resources, the model is designed to test and search the solution space of millions of possible retrofit and upgrade options for the group, arriving at the optimal use of these resources, to achieve the highest reduction of carbon consumption or the highest return on resource investment. It is a comprehensive decision process that incorporates carbon tracking, building energy analysis, design and planning optimisation, resource modelling and a 3-D graphic environment.

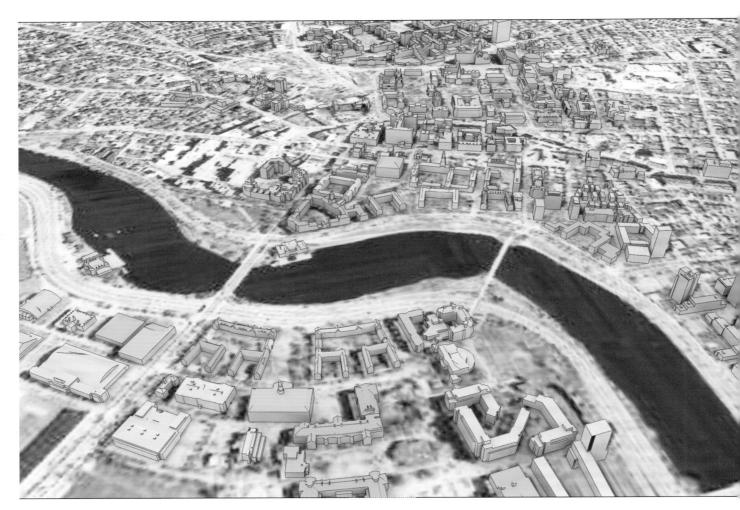

Daniel Segraves, Urban Energy Data Model, Academic Campus, 2011
Academic campuses such as this one, coloured by energy use intensity,
behave as organisms perhaps more so than urban districts because of their
tendency to utilise integrated, multi-structure systems.

*A legitimate working model of the city
must have the ability to compile, in some
useful capacity, a numeric representation
of all flows and entities – all the
movements throughout all of the avenues,
all the physical compositions of its parts,
all the means of production, atmospheric
conditions and fluctuations.*

Historic, current and projected impact is analysed by
applying various building energy analysis methods, using
collected local and city data such as building morphology,
facade construction, mechanical system, occupancy type,
population, urban surface make-up and so on. Under the realm
of 'projected impact', the model calculates the energy-related
impact of retrofit possibilities for the test subject, as well as
the resource implications of such retrofits. An optimisation
algorithm is implemented to allow three primary input-output
scenarios. First, given the anticipated or available resources,
the model finds the best allocation of this funding for optimal
impact reduction or optimal return on investment. Second,
given the desired energy savings, either as a specific value
or percentage, or by a particular code or initiative to comply
with, for example, LEED, BREEAM or the Living Building
Challenge, it finds the optimal retrofits and associated
resource expenditures needed to achieve this. A third input-
output scenario would enable finite testing on the impact of
specific retrofit options, foregoing the use of the optimisation
module. For the first two input-output scenarios, the optimal
target is determined by applying an evolutionary algorithm
which searches the extremely large solution space of possible
retrofit variations, testing each for energy and financial viability
against the criteria set.

Data

Analyses and decision processes aside, data is the ultimate currency in this endeavour. A legitimate working model of the city must have the ability to compile, in some useful capacity, a numeric representation of all flows and entities – all the movements throughout all of the avenues, all the physical compositions of its parts, all the means of production, atmospheric conditions and fluctuations. Such a complete set of data would require the development of a region-wide, extensive and intensive sensory system. The proportions of this development can only be seen as daunting, and prove that data collection is by far the most challenging aspect of this model. This poses a strong argument for decentralised sensing and intelligence, as is the preferred solution among natural systems. Indeed, it implies that the intelligence of the model proposed here should be enacted locally by all structures and participating agents, just as the intelligence of an organism is distributed via the genome. A proposal for a top-down decision model of the city may therefore, ironically, resolve itself as a firmly local conception. ⌂

Daniel Segraves, Urban Energy Data Model, Chicago Loop, 2011
above: The age of each building, represented here with darker colouring for older buildings, plays an important role in predicting the mechanical, structural and envelope make-up of the structure for the purpose of accelerated energy modelling.

below: Building morphology plays a crucial role in the energy of the building as well as the urban system as a whole, especially its effect on solar gain and shading, shown here as a heat map of sorts.

Colin Fournier

THE CITY BEYOND ANALOGY

COUNTERPOINT 04/2013 № 224

Is the city really all that complex? Can urban social behaviour be explained in the evolutionary drama of cross-species competition? Is urban self-organisation in fact the urban norm? Is the emphasis on systems that the 'system city' tag conjures up unduly restrictive? **Colin Fournier**, Emeritus Professor of Architecture and Urbanism at the Bartlett School of Architecture, University College London (UCL), prods and probes the precepts behind the *System City* issue, while being simultaneously fascinated and enthralled by it.

The thread that holds together the various articles in this issue is the commonly held view that cities are complex systems and that, as they grow larger in size, change faster and become increasingly sentient, the conceptual models and analytical tools we use to understand them – and to intervene within them – need to become more sophisticated, to learn from analogies with natural ecosystems and perhaps to adopt some analytical and modelling methods borrowed from other fields dealing with complexity.

The essays do not attempt to define a model for 'system city', but to open up the question as to what the elaboration of such a model may require, which is a particularly difficult question, since the 'law of requisite variety' states, in essence, that the models used to describe and control a system have to exhibit at least the same 'degree of variety' as the system under observation. The implication of this fundamental law of cybernetics – which is also an integral part of complexity theory – is that the universe of discourse that a comprehensive urban model has to embrace must be extremely broad, perhaps broader than the one that has so far been suggested by the authors.

Colin Fournier, *The city equation*, 2013
Both in academe and in professional practice, the presentation of an
elegantly concise algorithm to account for the dynamics of complex
urban systems at times begs for a suspension of disbelief.

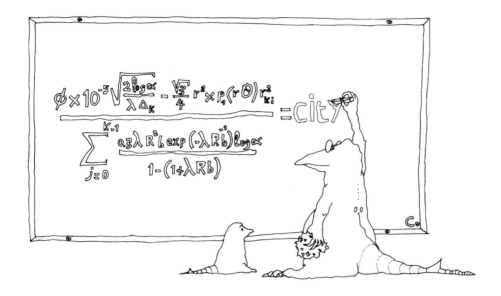

For a start, it has to include, geographically and conceptually, not only the city itself, but also its antithesis. The implicit assumption in the texts is that urbanisation will continue to increase exponentially, and that the problems that come with it will therefore have to be solved within the realm of the city alone. However, since urbanisation is a relatively recent historical phenomenon, and since most of the ecological and social disfunctions of the planet have resulted from the massive rural migrations first triggered by the Industrial Revolution and now further exacerbated in the post-industrial world, it would be wise, if the model is to be able to test alternatives, to consider the whole surface of the planet as our universe and to allow urban models to explore equally scenarios of decentralisation as well as those of further urbanisation.

The authors declare their intention to depart from the 'machine metaphors' of Modernism, but adopt in their stead two familiar biological metaphors that are equally reductionist: that of the termite hill and that of the forest. Analogies between cities and the edifices of social insects are misleading in that, both in terms of social organisation and physical structure, the hills of ants and termites present levels of complexity that are trivial in relation to those of even the simplest of human habitats. As for forests, the analysis carried out by Evan Greenberg and George Jeronimidis (pp 24–31) and their exposé of design implications applied, by analogy, to hyperdense 3-D urbanism, are highly pertinent. But again, urban social behaviour is far more complex than the co-evolutionary drama of cross-species competition even within the densest recesses of the Amazonian forest. So why bother with biological metaphors?

One of the persuasive reasons put forward in the text is that they help to understand the transformative power of 'self-organisation' in the evolution of complex systems and, by extension, the principles of 'emergence', both architecturally fashionable terms borrowed from other disciplines, and presented here as the next 'paradigm shift' that cities – and the models that describe them – might soon adopt. But cities have always been self-organised. They are the result of myriads of micro-economic decisions made by individual agents who are every bit as blind with respect to the overall implications of their actions as termites are. The major part of the exponential urban growth that is taking place globally is

Street in Central District, Hong Kong, from the Mid-Levels escalator
When all digitised systems become virtual and the 'city of bits' shifts to cyberspace, where will fruit, vegetables and flowers be offered and exchanged? Will there still be streets? Will red cabs still drop off their cargo of illicit couples in the middle of the night? Will there still be nights?

Escalator (the longest in the world?) at Langham Place shopping mall, Mong Kok, Hong Kong
opposite: In contemporary urban systems, the distinction between 'residence' and 'infrastructure' is becoming blurred. In Hong Kong they are merging: items of infrastructure become places, and buildings become part of the ubiquitous movement system, no less so than Mass Transit Railway (MTR) trains, cargo ships, ferries, buses, minibuses, trams, taxis, lifts and upper-level pedestrian walkways.

in so-called 'informal' settlements. Top-down planning is the exception and, throughout history, always has been. Self-organisation is the norm. It does not have to be invented; it is not the next conceptual and methodological horizon that the system city and its urban design models might have to aspire to reach: it is with us already. Self-organised urbanisation processes have to be observed and, if possible, tweaked to yield results that are more efficient, more environmentally sustainable and more socially equitable than they are now.

Given this prevalence of self-organised processes, it is clear that, in order to be robust, an urban model has to incorporate a multiplicity of perspectives and viewpoints. The title *System City* seems, in this context, with its emphasis on a coherent systemic view, to be unduly restrictive. It has led several of the authors to adopt, perhaps unintentionally, a discourse that belongs to the systems engineer rather than to any other discipline, let alone to the non-professional user. The language adopts by default the positivistic tone of Modernism, with remnants of top-down determinism that are at odds with the overall philosophical argument. It recalls the agenda

and dominant discourse of institutionalised decision makers, those called upon to make comprehensive masterplans, to develop 'all-knowing', quasi-Orwellian operational models that will observe the city and the flows through its interconnected infrastructure systems in order to facilitate their control, rather than a more pluralistic discourse addressing topics other than the systemic and allowing different voices to be expressed.

There are few references to broader cultural values beyond instrumental ones: the word 'aesthetics' is mentioned only twice (once in a pejorative way), and the words 'art', 'poetry' and 'emotion' never come up at all, which suggests that the more subjective or deviant readings of the city, even mildly marginal interpretations such as the psycho-geographic sensitivity of the Situationists, might not find a place in this rather pragmatic formulation of the model in gestation. However, thanks to the diversity of authors, the publication nevertheless contains its own radical counterpoints. The beautifully written text by Liam Young and Kate Davies (pp 38–45), exploring with forensic precision the outermost tentacular extensions of global capital's relentless supply chains, is a piece of pure surreal poetry transporting us magically to the edges of the known world. And the 'Third Natures' text by Cristina Díaz Moreno and Efrén García Grinda (pp 46–55, encouraging us to 'abandon the languages associated with the architecture of the city', to adopt an 'afterpop' language that would celebrate 'pleasure, creativity and political resistance in an explosion of collective cultural impatience' is a refreshingly subversive piece of writing. Therefore, there cannot be just one urban model, based on a perception of the city as 'system', but many competing models, to account for diverse socioeconomic, cultural and political backgrounds, including the renegade ones. The design model needs to be a collage of models, just as Colin Rowe and Fred Koetter, in their seminal book *Collage City* (1978)[1] stressed the importance of architectural diversity within the city as an antidote to generic reductionism.

The industrial–age machines that fascinated us in the 19th and 20th centuries with their steam engines, cogs and pistons have now been replaced by the massive server farms of multinationals such as Google, so that the machines have changed: giant supercomputers and the artificial intelligence protocols necessary to navigate immensely large amounts of data have become our new metaphors, those that are now beginning to haunt us.

We have not yet transcended the machine metaphors of Modernism. The industrial-age machines that fascinated us in the 19th and 20th centuries with their steam engines, cogs and pistons have now been replaced by the massive server farms of multinationals such as Google, so that the machines have changed: giant supercomputers and the artificial intelligence protocols necessary to navigate immensely large amounts of data have become our new metaphors, those that are now beginning to haunt us. The biological analogies we still refer to, nostalgic anecdotes of termite hills and rainforests, are just accompanying epiphenomena.

Daniel Segraves (pp 120–23) is right in assuming, by analogy with parallel computing, that the intelligence of the system city will be a distributed one. Above all, it will be large, as Jorge Luis Borges anticipated poetically in his parable of 'The Map and the Territory',[2] so large that the model might paradoxically end up merging with reality itself. Indeed, if it takes thousands of lines of code to even approximately simulate the parameters and variables coming into play in a very simple event, such as 'dog catches ball', think about the amount of coding that would be required to do justice to the life of the city. We will also have to accept that the model will be somewhat messy: as Stuart Kauffman has demonstrated, it is in the nature of complex systems to survive by maintaining themselves 'on the edge of Chaos',[3] exhibiting only just enough structure to ensure their continued existence, but enough blurred edges to allow for change.

Not only will the model be large, distributed and messy, but, more importantly from a philosophical point of view, we will have to accept that its internal logic will gradually escape our understanding. As Karl Sims found out when he developed relatively simple evolutionary algorithms to simulate movement in artificial creatures, there is a point when the internal chains of cause and effect that have led to a desired outcome will totally escape

Public housing in the New Territories, Hong Kong
How to address exponentially large numbers without the
impoverishment of endless repetition? Modernism failed,
Postmodernism just toyed with the question. Would Colin
Rowe's and Fred Koetter's *Collage City* model satisfy
cybernetics' 'law of requisite variety', or are more radical
forms of self-organisation required, to the point of giving
up control?

Hong Kong Island and Kowloon, from The Peak
The 'bottom-up' self-organisation principles of 'pure'
laissez-faire capitalism are the forces that shaped the
great cities of the world, both formal and informal, giving
complexity and variety to their urban cores and central
business districts. The shift to monopoly capital and now
to globalisation is reducing the 'quantity of variety' of the
urban system.

*The city is more than any
definition one may attempt
to offer, because of the vast
unknown that still lies beyond
the reach of its predatory
infrastructure systems.*

Notes
1. Colin Rowe and Fred Koetter, *Collage City*, MIT Press (Cambridge, MA), 1978.
2. Jorge Luis Borges, 'On Exactitude in Science' (original title 'Del rigor en la ciencia'), in *A Universal History of Infamy*, trans Norman Thomas de Giovanni, Penguin Books (London), 1975.
3. Stuart A Kauffman, *The Origins of Order: Self-Organization and Selection in Evolution*, Oxford University Press (New York), 1993.
4. Karl Sims, 'Evolving Virtual Creatures', 1994: see http://www.karlsims.com/papers/siggraph94.pdf.
5. Kevin Kelly, *Out of Control: The New Biology of Machines, Social Systems, and the Economic World*, Basic Books (New York), 1995.
6. Joseph Conrad, *Heart of Darkness*, Penguin Classics (London), 2012.
7. Arthur Rimbaud, *Illuminations*, WW Norton & Company (New York), 2012 (first published in 1886), and Antonin Artaud, *The Theatre of Cruelty*, Grove Press/Atlantic Monthly Press (New York), 1994 (first published in 1938).

and and sea, Causeway Bay Pier, Hong Kong Island
afe anchorage, a place for ships to moor: the economic liquidity
Hong Kong originated from sea trade. Without the firepower of
e British fleet, the dirty opium wars would not have secured the
mpire's fortunes. But the sea remains untamed: it is the constant
esence of the unknown lapping at the city's edge.

us.[4] Even if the system city does what we want it to do – assuming, that is, that we do know what we want it to do – we will have to come to terms with the fact that we no longer understand how it does it and that it has, in effect, become a 'black box', vanishing beneath our level of consciousness. We will have to accept that we are 'out of control', to paraphrase Kevin Kelly,[5] whoever 'we' may be. Once the system city and its model become fully sentient, we will enter the narratives that mythology and fiction have anticipated a long time ago: the Greek myth of Prometheus stealing fire from the Gods, the fatal stories of the Golem, of Frankenstein, of Jean-Luc Godard's intelligent but desolate *Alphaville* (1965), leading to the pathetic and prophetic revolt of Stanley Kubrick's HAL (Heuristically programmed ALgorithmic computer) in *2001: A Space Odyssey* (1968).

To read the city involves a journey beyond its comforts and into uncharted territories, both within and without. This issue's guest-editor informs us, in his biography, that, after reading Joseph Conrad, he went off to sea, and it seems that there are also explicit echoes of *Heart of Darkness* (1899)[6] in the turbulent voyages of the Unknown Fields Division (pp 38–45). The question is how far to follow Conrad, and which character to

identify with: to take Francis Ford Coppola's cinematic version (1991), do we follow Martin Sheen, the obedient agent from System City, dispatched as a hired assassin to make sure that its rational and ethical rules are respected and to terminate the deviant general, or do we follow Marlon Brando, its original extraordinary agent, prepared, at the cost of his life, to explore the city's dark edges? Few 'models' of understanding are prepared to go that far into the 'theatre of cruelty', even if it may mean not coming back, with the exception, perhaps, of Arthur Rimbaud and Antonin Artaud.[7]

Our search to understand the city is driven by an idealised desire to improve it, to make it less cruel. Despite the lessons of history, we are not prepared to perceive the city as nothing but the process and product of the exploitation of man by man, and of nature by man. Neither are we prepared to see it as a system, because systems, unlike humans, have a fixed programmatic purpose. The city is more than any definition one may attempt to offer, because of the vast unknown that still lies beyond the reach of its predatory infrastructure systems. ⌂

Francis Aish is a Partner and Head of Applied Research + Development at Foster + Partners. He studied aerospace systems engineering at the University of Southampton, and is currently completing an engineering doctorate at University College London (UCL). At Foster + Partners he leads the research and development of computational systems to model and solve complex, multidisciplinary design problems. In the course of this work he has been involved in over 200 projects and competitions, including the Swiss Re Headquarters, the Smithsonian Institution and Beijing International Airport.

Keith Besserud is the director of BlackBox, a research-oriented computational design resource within the Chicago office of Skidmore, Owings & Merrill (SOM). With design partner Ross Wimer, he set up the BlackBox studio in 2007 to lead the development and integration of advanced computational concepts within the multidisciplinary design processes of the office. In particular the group is interested in exploiting various types and sources of data to guide form-finding design processes. Within this approach the group relies on parametric frameworks built with scripting expertise and parametric software, as well as a variety of simulation and search optimisation tools, including those that are commercially available as well as those that are custom-developed by the team.

Joan Busquets is Professor at the Graduate School of Design (GSD), Harvard University. Prior to joining the GSD he was Professor in the School of Architecture at the Polytechnic University of Barcelona until 2002. He served as Head of Urban Planning for the Barcelona City Council from 1983 to 1989, and in the preparations for the Barcelona Olympics in 1992, including the New Downtowns for the City programme and the improvement process for existing neighbourhoods. He has also participated in strategic urban planning and design for the cities of Den Haag, Lisbon, Shanghai, Toulouse, Ningbo, Toledo and Delft.

Eva Castro has been teaching at the Architectural Association (AA) in London since 2003, and is also cofounder of Plasma Studio and Groundlab. She studied architecture and urbanism at the Universidad Central de Venezuela, and subsequently completed the AA Graduate Design programme with Jeff Kipnis. She is the winner of the Next Generation Architects Award, and the Young Architect of the Year, ContractWorld and the HotDip Galvanising awards. Her work is published and exhibited worldwide.

Kate Davies is a designer, writer and educator, and founder of the multidisciplinary group LiquidFactory. She creates objects, texts and drawings that deal with obscure territories of occupation. Her work explores the psychological aspects of extreme landscapes and notions of wilderness. She teaches diploma architecture courses at the Bartlett School of Architecture, UCL, and the Architecural Association, and is co-founder of the nomadic design studio the Unknown Fields Division based at the AA.

Adam Davis is an associate partner in Foster + Partners' Applied Research + Development group and an engineering doctorate candidate in the Virtual Environments, Imaging and Visualisation programme at UCL. He is currently investigating the use of machine learning to understand and simulate perception of the built environment. He has taught parametric and computational design at the University of Pennsylvania, Cornell University and the AA, and has been a tutor and organiser for SmartGeometry workshops and symposia in Delft and Barcelona.

Cristina Díaz Moreno and Efrén García Grinda are both architects and founders of the Madrid-based office AMID.cero9, and unit masters in Diploma 5 at the AA. Since 1998 they have been visiting teachers and lecturers profusely throughout the US, Europe and Asia and recently they have been appointed Professors in the Akademic der Bildenden Künst of Vienna. They have won more than 30 prizes in national and international competitions, and their projects have been widely disseminated not only in exhibitions and publications of architecture, but also in museums.

Phil Enquist is leader of the global city design practice of SOM, the world's most highly awarded urban planning group. He and his studios have improved the quality and efficiency of city living on five continents by creating location-unique strategic designs that integrate nature and urban density within a framework of future-focused public infrastructure. The scale of his design perspective continues to expand from innovating sustainable urban forms that enhance city living with walkable, transit-enabled districts humanised by their natural amenities to rapidly changing urban clusters within regional ecosystems like North America's Great Lakes basin and China's Bohai Rim.

Colin Fournier was educated at the AA in London. He is Emeritus Professor of Architecture and Urbanism at the Bartlett School of Architecture, UCL, where he was Director of the MArch in Urban Design, and is currently a visiting professor at the Chinese University of Hong Kong (CUHK). He was an associate member of Archigram Architects, and Planning Director of the Parsons Company in Pasadena, California, implementing urban

design projects in the Middle East, in particular the new town of Yanbu in Saudi Arabia. He was Bernard Tschumi's partner for the design of the Parc de la Villette in Paris, and co-author, with Sir Peter Cook, of the Graz Kunsthaus in Austria. His recently completed project, Open Cinema, was built in Guimarães, Portugal. He is a partner of the TETRA architectural practice based in Hong Kong.

Mehran Gharleghi received his BA from Tehran University of Science and Technology and MArch from the Emergent Technologies and Design (EmTech) programme at the AA. His research has won international awards such as the AA Fab Research Cluster Symposium 2009 and International Prize for Sustainable Architecture 2010. He is now an EmTech course tutor, and co-founder and director of studioINTEGRATE, an international architectural studio based in London.

Evan Greenberg is a researcher and design consultant investigating biomimicry, advanced fabrication processes, and the behaviour of responsive and distributed systems across a range of scales from product design to architecture and urban design. He has worked with architects, engineers, artists and fashion designers and has lectured and taught around the world. He is Studio Master in the EmTech programme at the AA where he graduated with distinction in 2007.

Craig Hartman is a design partner based in SOM's San Francisco Office. His work with SOM in the US, Europe and Asia, while extremely broad in its typology – ranging from entire urban districts to singular works of commercial, civic and cultural architecture – consistently adheres to a rigorous modern vocabulary that acknowledges issues of place involving climate, physical and cultural landscape, and historic precedent. His work has been recognised with over 120 awards for design, which, in addition to eight national AIA Honor Awards, includes two Gold LEED certifications and AIA awards for environmental sustainability at Treasure Island and the University of California, Merced. He also received a Federal Design Achievement Award in the 2000 Presidential Design Awards Program.

George Jeronimidis has authored more than a hundred papers, conference proceedings and book contributions in the fields of biomechanics, biomimetics, composite mechanics, smart materials and structures, and bio-inspired technologies. In 1992, along with Professor Julian Vincent, he set up the Centre for Biomimetics at the University of Reading, one of the first truly interdisciplinary research centres across biological and engineering disciplines. He is co-director of the Emergent Technologies and Design

(EmTech) programme at the AA, a visiting professor at the Dipartmento di Architettura e Urbanistica at the Politecnico di Bari, President of BIOKON International, and a member of the Scientific Advisory Board of the Max Planck Institute of Colloids and Interfaces.

Marina Lathouri, an architect and critic, directs the graduate programme in History and Critical Thinking at the AA and is a visiting lecturer at the University of Cambridge. She has taught at the University of Pennsylvania and presently collaborates with the University of Navarra in Spain. She was recently appointed Distinguished Visiting Professor at the Universidad Católica in Santiago, Chile. Her current research interests lie in the conjunction of urban theory and political philosophy. Most recently, she co-authored the book *Intimate Metropolis: Urban Subjects in the Modern City* (Routledge, 2009) and has also published several articles.

Wolf Mangelsdorf was born and grew up in Germany. He studied architecture and civil engineering at Karlsruhe University, where he also worked for an architectural practice after graduation. After a research stay at Kyoto University he moved to the UK in 1997 to work as a structural engineer at Anthony Hunt Associates in its Cirencester and London offices. Since 2002 he has been with Buro Happold in London where he is a partner,

responsible for structural engineering and leading the London structures team. He is a project principal for a wide range of multidisciplinary projects internationally and in the UK, working with leading architects. He has a design-focused approach to his project work with strong expertise in the development of complex geometries and form-defined structures, as well as multidisciplinary design and integration. He has been teaching at the AA since 2000, where he is part of the EmTech programme. He has been a guest lecturer and guest tutor at universities internationally.

José Alfredo Ramírez is an architect and founding director of Groundlab. He studied architecture in Mexico City, and the AA Landscape Urbanism graduate programme in 2005. At Groundlab he has won a number of competitions, including the Longgang City international competition masterplan and the international horticultural exhibition project in Xian. He co-directs the AA Landscape Urbanism programme and is the Director of the AA Mexico City Visiting School. He has lectured worldwide on landscape urbanism and on the work of Groundlab.

Eduardo Rico is a civil engineer and MA Landscape Urbanism graduate currently working at Arup. He is currently engaged

in strategic advice on infrastructure and transportation for urban masterplanning in Arup's ILG team, and research in the contemporary design practices feeding infrastructural inputs into architectural urbanism. He co-directs the AA Landscape Urbanism programme and is also a member of design practices such as Groundlab and Relational Urbanism.

Mark Sarkisian is Director of Structural Engineering at SOM. He has developed engineering solutions for over a hundred building projects around the world, including some of the tallest and most complex. He holds six US patents, including patents for four high-performance seismic structural mechanisms and two for seismic and environmentally responsible structural systems. He is the author of *Designing Tall Buildings: Structure as Architecture* (Routledge, 2011), and teaches at the University of California, Berkeley, California College of the Arts, Stanford University and Cal Poly. He has a BS-CE degree from the University of Connecticut, and an MS-SE from Lehigh University, and is a Fellow of the Academy of Distinguished Engineers.

Daniel Segraves is a specialist in advanced modelling and computational design strategies, with expertise spanning a wide spectrum from architectural systems optimisation to urban energy modelling. His interest lies in the development of man-made things with the efficiency, intelligence and beauty found only in natural systems. Since earning his Master of Architecture at the AA (EmTech) programme, he has worked as computational design researcher or consultant for Adrian Smith + Gordon Gill Architecture, OMA (Rotterdam office), Arup (London office), Ross Lovegrove Studio (London) and X-Architects (Dubai). He currently works for Gensler. His work and writing has been published in *Detail*, *∆*, *Architectural Record*, *Dwell* and others.

Jack Self is a London-based architect, theorist and writer. He regularly contributes to a number of publications, including the *Architectural Review* and *Building Design*. He is Founding Editor of the AA's weekly publication *Fulcrum*, and Associate Editor at Strelka Press. He recently completed an MA in philosophy, investigating morality and neoliberal economic theory, which is also the principal field of his architectural design work.

Ricard V Solé is ICREA research professor at the Universitat Pompeu Fabra where he leads the Complex Systems Lab. He is also external professor of the Santa Fe Institute, New Mexico. He explores the origins and evolution of complexity in both natural and artificial systems, searching for potential universal patterns of organisation. He has published more than 200 papers in peer-reviewed journals, and several books, including *Signs of Life: How Complexity Pervades Biology*, with Brian Goodwin (Basic Books, 2001) and *Phase Transitions* (Princeton University Press, 2011).

Iain D Stewart is postdoctoral fellow in the Department of Geography, University of British Columbia. He is a specialist in urban effects on climate, and particularly the heat island effect. His research addresses methodological issues in heat island studies, and encourages critical thinking on literature quality and urban climate reporting. His current focus is the thermal and structural classification of cities, and the development of international protocols for heat island observations.

Martha Tsigkari is an associate partner at Foster + Partners' Applied Research + Development group, where she creates and develops generative design systems within the context of geometrically and programmatically challenging international projects. She also holds a tutor's position at the Bartlett, UCL, where she teaches programming to graduate students, and participates as a tutor and presenter in conferences and workshops internationally.

Her interest lies in incorporating parametric design and scripting techniques to produce custom tools that are then used for testing design methods and managing workflows.

Sergi Valverde is a visiting professor at the Universitat Pompeu Fabra, and a member of the ICREA-Complex Systems Lab and the Institute of Evolutionary Biology (CSIC-UPF) in Barcelona. He received a degree in computer science and a PhD in applied physics from the Universitat Politècnica de Catalunya. His research explores the origins of innovation in artificial systems and their implications for biological systems. He has published more than 40 papers in peer-review journals, including *Nature Biotechnology* and *Proceedings of the National Academy of Sciences (PNAS)*.

Liam Young is an architect who operates in the spaces between design, fiction and futures. He is founder of the think tank Tomorrow's Thoughts Today, a group whose work explores the possibilities of fantastic, speculative and imaginary urbanisms. He also runs a graduate studio at Princeton, and is co-founder of the Unknown Fields Division, a nomadic studio based at the AA in London that travels on biannual expeditions to the ends of the earth to investigate extreme landscapes, alien terrains and industrial ecologies. His projects develop fictional speculations as critical instruments to survey the consequences of emerging environmental and technological futures.

INDIVIDUAL BACKLIST ISSUES OF △D ARE AVAILABLE FOR PURCHASE AT £24.99 / US$45

TO ORDER AND SUBSCRIBE SEE BELOW

What is *Architectural Design*?

Founded in 1930, *Architectural Design* (△D) is an influential and prestigious publication. It combines the currency and topicality of a newsstand journal with the rigour and production qualities of a book. With an almost unrivalled reputation worldwide, it is consistently at the forefront of cultural thought and design.

Each title of △D is edited by an invited guest-editor, who is an international expert in the field. Renowned for being at the leading edge of design and new technologies, △D also covers themes as diverse as architectural history, the environment, interior design, landscape architecture and urban design.

Provocative and inspirational, △D inspires theoretical, creative and technological advances. It questions the outcome of technical innovations as well as the far-reaching social, cultural and environmental challenges that present themselves today.

For further information on △D, subscriptions and purchasing single issues see: www.architectural-design-magazine.com

How to Subscribe
With 6 issues a year, you can subscribe to △D (either print, online or through the △D App for iPad).

INSTITUTIONAL SUBSCRIPTION
£212/US$398 print or online

INSTITUTIONAL SUBSCRIPTION
£244/US$457 combined print & online

PERSONAL-RATE SUBSCRIPTION
£120/US$189 print and iPad access

STUDENT-RATE SUBSCRIPTION
£75/US$117 print only

To subscribe to print or online:
Tel: +44 (0) 1243 843 272
Email: cs-journals@wiley.com

△D APP FOR iPAD
For information on the △D App for iPad go to www.architectural-design-magazine.com
6-issue subscription: £44.99/US$64.99
Individual issue: £9.99/US$13.99

SCARCITY
ARCHITECTURE IN AN AGE OF DEPLETING RESOURCES

Volume 82 No 4
ISBN 978 1119 973621

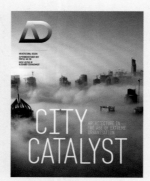

CITY CATALYST

Volume 82 No 5
ISBN 978 1119 972662

HUMAN EXPERIENCE AND PLACE
SUSTAINING IDENTITY

Volume 82 No 6
ISBN 978 1118 336410

THE INNOVATION IMPERATIVE
ARCHITECTURES OF VITALITY

Volume 83 No 1
ISBN 978 1119 978657

COMPUTATION WORKS
THE BUILDING OF ALGORITHMIC THOUGHT

Volume 83 No 2
ISBN 978 1119 952862

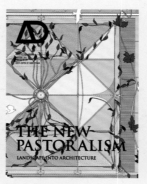

THE NEW PASTORALISM
LANDSCAPE INTO ARCHITECTURE

Volume 83 No 3
ISBN 978 1118 336984

NOW available on the iPad!

- Buy single issues or subscribe
- Store all downloaded issues to your personal library
- Easily navigable format brings new life to AD articles
- Free to personal print subscribers

Available on the App Store